SHAKESPEARE MEETS THE BUDDHA

Shakespeare's Words Illustrate Buddhist Teachings

Edward Dickey

TABLE OF CONTENTS

Preface:

A Meeting of Minds

L ET US IMAGINE that we could bring the Buddha and Shakespeare together for a meeting of minds. We picture them on a mild spring afternoon in an open pavilion overlooking a grove of blossoming cherry trees. Shakespeare would arrive wearing a wide lace-trimmed collar, doublet, and hose and find the Buddha in robes made from squares of saffron-colored cloth. Shakespeare would see wisdom and compassion in the Buddha's eyes, and the Buddha would see open attention in Shakespeare's face. They would each bow, recognizing the other as a great being.

In preparation for their meeting, the Buddha would have read most of the plays and several sonnets, and Shakespeare would have read *The Dhammapada (Way of Truth)*, two or three sutras, and a life of the Buddha. While reading the plays, the Buddha's heart would overflow with compassion for the suffering of the poor, deluded characters. And in the Buddha's teachings, Shakespeare would find the profound stillness that lies beneath the storms of life, storms so well depicted in his plays.

They would soon settle into a discussion, with thoughtful questions, careful explanations, moments of puzzlement, and occasional nods of agreement. What would their conversation cover? It might include the mind, suffering and its causes, selfless concern for others, impermanence and death, illusion and awakening, actions and their consequences, and the nature of the self. It would be a conversation worth hearing.

Alas, Shakespeare and the Buddha, separated in time and space by more than 2,000 years and 4,700 miles, could never have met in person. But they can meet in the mind of anyone who cares to make the connection. As we will see in the following pages, the West's greatest poetry sometimes resonates with the East's most profound spiritual teaching.

Disclaimer

I HAVE TRIED TO find Buddhist teachings that can be related to Shakespeare's works and passages from Shakespeare that can be related to Buddhist teachings. What I have found is considerable but amounts to a fraction of Buddhism and a fraction of Shakespeare.

The Buddha is said to have given 84,000 teachings to counter 84,000 obscurations that afflict sentient beings. Whatever the actual number of teachings, we know that the Buddhist Dharma is vast, with several hundred sutras and many more commentaries. This book focuses on a few essential points common to most schools of Buddhism. But it does not cover all aspects of any Buddhist path and does not pretend to cover the more specialized or advanced aspects of Buddhist teaching. See the reading suggestions at the end for Buddhist teachings and practice advice from teachers in the Theravadin, Tibetan, and Zen Buddhist traditions.

Shakespeare Meets the Buddha is written for the the Shakespeare lover curious about Buddhism, for the Buddhist with an interest in Shakespeare, and for the generalist with an interest in both. And it is for anyone who enjoys finding comparable expressions of universal truths in widely different eras, lands, and cultures.

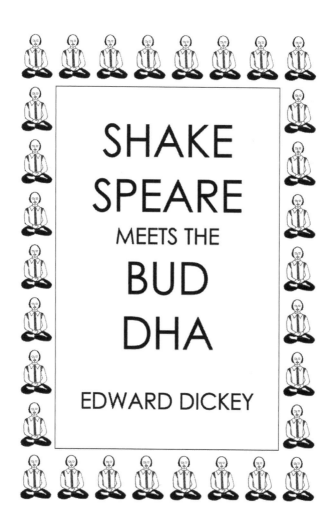

SHAKE SPEARE

MEETS THE

BUD DHA

EDWARD DICKEY

1

Across a Great Divide

SEVERAL YEARS AGO, I spent two weeks at a Buddhist meditation retreat in the highlands of south-central France. Our teachings and practices took place in a large white canvas tent, with sides drawn up to let in the summer breeze. From the tent, we saw colorful Tibetan prayer flags moving with the wind, heard delivery trucks bringing food and supplies, and smelled the vegetable curry prepared for lunch.

Our morning and afternoon sessions each began and ended with a prayer for the benefit of all beings. Periods of meditation were interspersed with teachings, short breaks, and a longer break at noon. Except for mantra recitation, we observed silence for the ten hours between breakfast and dinner.

Sitting up straight in meditation posture, relaxed and alert, and with eyes open, we endeavored to tame our minds by resting attention on a series of objects. We began with an image of the Buddha sitting serene and majestic at the moment of his enlightenment. We sought to emulate him as we followed our teacher's instruction to sit like a mountain, undisturbed by the weather around it. Then, after several minutes, we turned our attention to a mantra. We chanted, "Om Mani Padme Hung,"[1] and let the sacred syllables wash over and through us, dispelling negative thoughts and emotions. And after the last syllable died away, we sat in the stillness that followed. Inspired by the image of the Buddha and energized by mantra recitation, we then rested our attention on the breath, breathing naturally and relaxing the mind and body a little more with each outbreath.

Over the following days, we would go on to rest our attention on sounds, bodily sensations, and passing thoughts. In each case, our instructions were: (1) rest attention on the object; (2) watch the mind, and when attention wanders, gently return it to the object; and (3) otherwise, rest the mind in stillness. Finally, we let go of all objects and tried resting in awareness of awareness itself.

Outwardly, we may have appeared composed, but inwardly we struggled, some with distracting thoughts, some with strong emotions, some with back pain, some with strained knees, and some with drooping eyelids. When I should have been focusing on an object, I was often carried away by one thought after another:

> Why this nasal congestion? Do I have a cold or is it an allergy? I hope everything is alright at home. I could use some more coffee. The guy sitting next to me might be asleep. When are they going to ring the bell to end this session? I'm ready for lunch. Oops, I should be focusing on the breath. I'd better start over.

I was struggling with what Buddhists call a monkey mind. But our teacher assured us that distracting thoughts, emotions, and sensations were an inevitable part of the process and that noticing them was a sign of progress.

I would like to say that by the end of the retreat I had my distractions under control, but miracles do not happen in two weeks. I was, however, a little happier, a little more attentive, and at times a little calmer. There had been no "trippy" experiences, but such experiences were not the purpose of our meditation. The purpose was to let go of the unchecked thoughts and emotions that obscure our true nature, just as clouds obscure a clear blue sky. As I boarded the bus that would take me to the airport, I resolved to meditate regularly, spend less time lost in cloudy thoughts of the past and future, and spend more time in the clear blue sky of the present. [2]

. . .

Within twenty-four hours of my return to Washington, D.C., I attended a performance of *Othello* at our Shakespeare Theatre. I entered the theatre still feeling jet-lagged but was soon transfixed by the thoroughly absorbing production. Three hours later, after the scheming, deception, and manipulation, after the mental anguish, madness, and killing, and after the building tension and catastrophe, I gazed at the bodies of Desdemona, Emilia, and Othello lying on the stage. The emotions aroused in me had been exhausted, and I left the theatre with a tranquil feeling, somewhat like the feeling I had experienced as a beginning meditator.

In the days that followed, I thought of Shakespeare writing plays amid the bustle of crowded London and of the Buddha teaching in the deer park at Sarnath.[3] I had found each to be, in their own way, a source of great insight into the human condition, and I wondered if there were any parallels or instructive connections between Shakespeare's works and the Buddha's teachings.

I must have read a dozen books about the Buddha and Buddhism but found little that I could relate to Shakespeare. It was as if the Buddha and Shakespeare were from different planets. The Buddha taught his followers to transcend the cycle of birth, death, and rebirth by doing no harm, training the mind, and serving others. Shakespeare wrote plays and poems about romantic love, sex, war, royal power, betrayal, jealousy, murder, and revenge. The apparent lack of common ground should not have come as a surprise. Drama requires tension within and between individuals with negative emotions and conflicting desires. These essential ingredients of drama are the very things the Buddha taught his followers to overcome.

For Buddhists, human life is precious because

it provides the conditions needed to reach a state beyond worldly attachments and aversions. By contrast, Shakespeare is very much of this world, with all its suffering and happiness, strife and concord, malevolence, and nobility.

My search for connections was at an impasse, and before me loomed a chasm of historical, cultural, and religious differences between Shakespeare's England and the world of the Buddha. Concluding that the task was hopeless, I gave up. If there were relationships between such disparate realms, I would not be the one to find them. But as soon as I stopped searching, connections began to reveal themselves. Now that I was no longer trying, it gradually occurred to me that the Buddha and Shakespeare shared some basic understandings. For example, they both knew that:

- Happiness depends on the mind and our ability to control it.
- Suffering is an inescapable part of life.
- Selfless concern for others alleviates suffering.
- Life is fleeting and death unavoidable.
- What we take to be real is illusion.
- We can awaken from illusion.

- Attachment brings suffering, and non-attachment brings contentment.
- Ill-intentioned actions have bad consequences for the actor.
- Bad actions can be redeemed through remorse.
- The sense of self to which we cling is without intrinsic existence.

As the fog lifted, I began to find passages and dramatic situations in Shakespeare's works that illustrate some of the Buddha's basic teachings. But Shakespeare would have known nothing about the teachings of the Buddha. Knowledge of Buddhism would not reach England until after Shakespeare's lifetime. Believers in rebirth might speculate that Shakespeare was a bodhisattva, a being able to reach nirvana,[4] who chose instead to be reborn in Elizabethan England to spread Buddhist teachings in a new form to new audiences. But we don't have to believe that Shakespeare was a bodhisattva to understand how his works might sometimes resonate with the teachings of the Buddha. We have only to appreciate the universality of a writer whose plays have been translated into 80 languages and remained in continuous production for over 400 years.

2

Shakespeare's Vast Perspective

A S SHAKESPEARE'S FRIEND and fellow playwright, Ben Jonson, wrote, "He was not of an age, but for all time."[5] The poet Samuel Taylor Coleridge went farther, writing that Shakespeare "shakes off the iron bondage of space"[6] as well as time, to produce plays and poems "out of the unfathomable depths of his oceanic mind."[7]

Out of his oceanic mind, Shakespeare brought forth human experience in all its depth and variety. He shows us every feeling known to humankind, including love, compassion, joy, equanimity, sadness, grief, hatred, pride, ambition, jealousy, and remorse. He takes us inside the minds of lovers, deposed monarchs, jealous husbands, mistreated fathers, grieving parents, and serial killers. He places characters in extreme situations that test their limits and take some to the brink of madness and beyond. His settings include royal courts, taverns, battlefields, bone-strewn gravesides, blasted heaths, enchanted islands, and fairy-haunted forests. His characters encompass the royal and common, the merciful and ruthless, the benevolent and malign, the true and false, and the starry-eyed and world-weary. To describe Shakespeare, Coleridge coined the term "myriad-minded," which, according to the *Merriam-Webster Dictionary*, means that he had "a mind of extreme versatility and power."[8]

Ben Jonson recognized that Shakespeare transcends his time. In several of his sonnets, including *Sonnet 55*, Shakespeare announces his intention to do no less:

> *Not marble nor the gilded monuments*
> *Of princes shall outlive this powerful rhyme...*
> *Your praise shall still find room*
> *Even in the eyes of all posterity*
> *That wear this world out to the ending doom.*[9]

He intends for his poems to last not just for a long time, but "to the ending doom." He could have had similar aspirations for his plays. In

Julius Caesar, after the assassination of Caesar, Cassius asks:

> *How many ages hence*
> *Shall this our lofty scene be acted over*
> *In states unborn and accents yet un-*
> *known. (III.i.124-126)*

These words might describe Shakespeare's achievement as a playwright. He transcends the limits of his own time and place to write for audiences that will encounter his works in the distant future, "in states unborn and accents yet unknown." He writes for us and for the millions who have experienced his works over the last 400 years, and for those who will experience them from now until the ending doom.

Shakespeare welcomes everyone into his audience. His perspective is vast, but that of the Buddha is even vaster. The Buddha envisioned no less than the end of suffering and the ultimate enlightenment of all beings. Two such universal visions cannot be mutually exclusive, and any correspondences between them should be well worth exploring. Our journey of exploration will begin with the mind.

3

Mindfulness

ACCORDING TO JON KABAT-ZINN, founder of the Center for Mindfulness in Medicine:

Mindfulness is awareness that arises through paying attention, on purpose, in the present moment, nonjudgmentally [10]

Mindfulness is often cultivated through formal meditation, beginning with mindfulness of the breath. But it is even more important to be mindful as we go about our daily lives. Mindful attention to whatever is happening in the moment can itself be a kind of meditation, whether we are walking the dog, washing dishes, looking at flowers, watching birds, observing people, or noticing our thoughts and emotions as they arise and dissolve. The Buddha taught mindfulness and praised the mindful observer:

Mindful among the mindless,
Awake while others dream,
Swift as the racehorse,
He outstrips the field.[11]

The alternative to mindfulness is to be so in thrall to our thoughts and emotions, including memories, plans, hopes, fears, resentments, and worries, that we go through life on automatic pilot, unmindful of what we are doing or of what goes on around us. The problem is not the thoughts, which arise naturally. The problem is our tendency to let them take over our minds, with thought leading to though.t leading to thought. Before we know it, thoughts are triggering emotions, and we are lost in an endless cascade of distraction. Thus distracted, we are in the grip of a "monkey mind," jumping uncontrolled from one thought or emotion to the next.

Shakespeare knew all about the monkey mind. In *A Midsummer Night's Dream,* he writes of "lovers and madmen" with "seething brains." His plays contain many such characters, but he mastered his own mind well enough to create a body of work grounded in mindful observation of:

- natural surroundings,
- the personalities and behavior of others,
- and interior mental states.

Attention to natural surroundings would have come early as young Shakespeare explored the gardens, meadows, riverbanks, and forests around Stratford, observing the shapes, colors, movements, sounds, smells, and weather of the rural countryside. These experiences remained with him when he sat down to write poems and plays that contain references to 57 species of birds and 180 different flowers, weeds, trees, fruits, and vegetables, along with memorable evocations of weather. Consider this brief passage from The *Winter's Tale*:

> *Daffodils,*
> *That come before the swallow dares, and take*
> *The winds of March with beauty. (IV.iv.141-143).*

In fifteen short words, Shakespeare captures, with Zen-like economy, a vivid experience of nature. Or consider the opening lines of Gertrude's report of the drowning of Ophelia in *Hamlet*:

> *There is a willow grows askant [across] the brook*
> *That shows his hoary [white] leaves in the glassy*
> *stream. (IV.vii.190-191)*

The essayist, William Hazlitt, noted that:

> *The leaves of the willow are, in fact, white under-*
> *neath, and it is this part of them which would ap-*
> *pear "hoary" in the reflection of the brook.*[12]

In *Much Ado About Nothing,* three characters see their friend Beatrice trying to hide while eaves-dropping on their conversation. One says:

> *For look where Beatrice like a lapwing runs*
> *Close by the ground, to hear our conference.*
> *(III.i.1099-1100)*

The lapwing does indeed stay close to the ground, where it nests and feeds on worms and insects.[13] Details such as daffodils blowing in a cold March wind, or the white undersides of willow leaves reflected in water, or a lapwing running close to the ground reflect the author's mindful attention to nature.

Then there is his attention to the personalities and behavior of others. The title of an article in

14

Elephant Journal asserts that "People Watching is the New Meditation."[14] Whether or not people watching is the new meditation, careful attention to others is a form of mindfulness that Shakespeare must have practiced. We can imagine Shakespeare, the people watcher, observing those he encountered in the workshop, schoolroom, marketplace, church, or tavern. He noticed and remembered their moods, idiosyncrasies, and manners of speech, gathering a store of material that he would later use in creating such memorable characters as:

- the dissolute reprobate, Falstaff, of *Henry IV Parts 1 & 2* and *The Merry Wives of Windsor,*
- the garrulous Nurse of *Romeo and Juliet,*
- the vain and puritanical Malvolio of *Twelfth Night,*
- the drunken porter of *Macbeth,*
- the carefree Bottom the Weaver, of *A Midsummer Night's Dream,*
- the bumbling constable, Dogberry, of *Much Ado About Nothing,* and
- the meddling Polonius of *Hamlet.*

Drawing on his observations of human behavior, Shakespeare created over a thousand characters,[15] many of them as real to us as the people we know. He must have been one of the greatest people watchers of all time.

Still, people watching has limits. Observation of outer behavior may contribute to the creation of memorable characters, but some characters have an inner dimension that cannot be captured through exterior observation alone. Shakespeare takes us inside the minds of the love-struck Romeo and Juliet, the depressive Hamlet, the fragile Ophelia, the malevolent and scheming Iago, the tormented Othello, the psychopathic Richard III, the angry Lear sliding into madness, and the ruthless Macbeth, with his mind full of scorpions. How did Shakespeare imagine so vividly the varied inner lives of these and other characters?

In *Sonnet 109*, he writes of a nature inhabited by "all frailties that besiege all kinds of blood." Shakespeare must have drawn on his own mental states, the frailties and strengths within himself, to imagine the mental states of his characters. With a gift for mindful introspection and an all-encompassing imagination, he created characters that continue to fascinate us after more than 400 years.

We might liken the mind to an ocean and our uncontrolled thoughts and emotions to ceaselessly pounding waves. We can quiet those waves if we set aside resentments about the past and anxieties about the future and return to the still point of the present moment. In *The Tempest*, Shakespeare describes a comparable transformation. As the play begins, we hear the cries of mariners as their ship sinks in a raging sea. But in the next scene, a haunting air takes us from the stormy surface to the calm of the sea floor:

> *Full fathom five thy father lies.*
> *Of his bones are coral made.*
> *Those are pearls that were his eyes.*
> *Nothing of him that doth fade*
> *But doth suffer a sea change*
> *Into something rich and strange. (I.ii.474-479)*

By mindfully observing thoughts and emotions and learning to master them, we can bring about a sea change of the mind. Taming the mind is the subject of our next chapter.

4

Taming the Mind

T HE "FRAILTIES THAT BESIEGE all kinds of blood" give rise to thoughts and emotions that will control us if we do not learn to control them. As the Buddha teaches:

We are what we think.
All that we are arises with our thoughts.
With our thoughts we make the world.[16]

Hamlet testifies to the power of the mind to shape our experience when he tells his visiting fellow students, Rosencrantz and Guildenstern, that:

there is nothing either good or bad but thinking makes it so. (II.ii.268-269)

And:

*I could be bounded in a nutshell and count myself
a king of infinite space, were it not that I have bad
dreams. (II.ii.273-275)*

Hamlet's bad dreams arise from a mind that is
not yet tamed. Spiritual teachers have likened an
untamed mind to a glass of muddy water and a
tamed mind to a glass in which the mud has settled to the bottom and the water is clear. Shakespeare uses a similar analogy in *Troilus and Cressida* when he has Achilles say:

*My mind is troubled, like a fountain stirred,
And I myself see not the bottom of it. (III.iii.308-
309)*

Most of us rarely see to the bottom of our minds,
so much are they stirred by distracting thoughts
and emotions. But meditators can with practice
begin to tame their minds by watching thoughts
and emotions as they arise and noting them
without attachment or aversion as they pass. We
are not our thoughts and emotions, and the less
we identify with them, the clearer our minds
will be. With clearer minds, we can find a little
space between a stimulus, such as a perceived
insult, and the negative thoughts and emotions
that may arise in response to it. In that space, we

can restrain thoughts and emotions that would otherwise consume us, knowing that they will fade and disappear if we don't give them our energy. Among the most dangerous emotions are jealousy, anger, and lust for power. If we habitually fall under their control, we will be sure to regret it. As the Buddha teaches:

Your worst enemy cannot harm you as much
As your own thoughts, unguarded.[17]

Although Shakespeare could not have been familiar with Buddhist meditation practices, his plays amply illustrate the Buddha's teaching about the perils of an unguarded mind.

Consider Othello. At the opening of the play, he has married Desdemona and faces the wrath of her father. But the Venetian state sides with Othello and sends him to defend Cyprus from a Turkish invasion. By the time he reaches Cyprus, a storm has destroyed the Turkish fleet, and his bride has arrived to join him. Everything goes well for Othello until the malevolent ensign, Iago, plants in his mind the false notion that Desdemona is committing adultery with Lieutenant Cassio. This inflammatory thought ignites the Moor's jealousy, and his mental state

20

rapidly deteriorates as Iago feeds the flames with misleading insinuations.

Even as Othello writhes in agony under the spell of jealousy, "the green-eyed monster," he knows that the cause of his anguish is his mind and not outer circumstances:

What sense had I of her stol'n hours of lust?
I saw't not, thought it not, it harm'd not me:
I slept the next night well, was free and merry;
I found not Cassio's kisses on her lips:
He that is robb'd, not wanting what is stol'n,
Let him not know't, and he's not robb'd at all...
(III.iii.389-395)

I had been happy, if the general camp,
Pioners and all, had tasted her sweet body,
So I had nothing known. O, now, forever
Farewell the tranquil mind! Farewell content!
(III.iii.397-400)

Manipulated by Iago and unable to control the emotions that are tearing him apart, Othello suffocates his wife and then learns of her innocence. Looking on her body, he laments:

Blow me about in winds, roast me in sulfur,
Wash me in steep-down gulfs of liquid fire!
(V.ii.330-331)

If any Shakespearean character suffers the torments of hell, it is Othello, who ends by stabbing himself to death. But it need not have come to that. Between the stimulus of Iago's lies and the response of all-consuming jealousy, there was a gap, a space in which Othello might have taken a deep breath, restrained his emotions, and stopped to think. With his emotions in check, he might have questioned whether there was time or opportunity for the alleged adultery. A more clearheaded Othello might then have seen through Iago's lies, or at least retained enough self-control not to kill his wife.

Then there is King Lear, who plans to enjoy a happy retirement after dividing his kingdom among three daughters. His plan gets off to a bad start when he asks his daughters:

Which of you shall we say doth love us most,
That we our largest bounty may extend
Where nature doth with merit challenge. (I.i.56-
58)

Two wicked daughters, Goneril and Regan, make dishonest declarations of love, but his youngest and best-loved child, Cordelia, can only say:

> *I love your Majesty*
> *According to my bond, no more nor less. (I.i.101-*
> *102)*

At this, the disappointed Lear gives way to rage and angrily disinherits Cordelia. He realizes his mistake too late when the wicked daughters gain power and begin to treat him slightingly, take away his retinue, and leave him out in a raging storm. Like Othello, he knows that his anguish is of the mind and is far worse than any physical torment:

> *Thou think'st 'tis much that this contentious*
> *storm*
> *Invades us to the skin: so 'tis to thee;*
> *But where the greater malady is fix'd,*
> *The lesser is scarce felt. Thou'ldst shun a bear;*
> *But if thy flight lay toward the raging sea,*
> *Thou'ldst meet the bear i' the mouth. When the*
> *mind's free,*
> *The body's delicate: the tempest in my mind*
> *Doth from my senses take all feeling else*

Save what beats there. Filial ingratitude! (III.iv.6-
14)

Lear's mental suffering continues long after the outward storm abates. When Cordelia returns and takes him into her care, he wakes to say:

Thou art a soul in bliss, but I am bound
Upon a wheel of fire, that mine own tears
Do scald like molten lead. (IV.vii.46-48)

Lear's mind, deluded by a lifetime of deference and flattery, is unprepared for harsh treatment. Under the weight of mental anguish too great to bear, he descends into madness. But the suffering and madness could have been avoided. Between the stimulus of disappointment and the response of blind rage, he had an opportunity to stop and observe his anger before being caught up in it. Had he taken that opportunity and thought for a moment, a more clearheaded Lear might have understood Cordelia's honesty and seen through his older daughters' deceit. He might then have reconsidered the whole plan and retained control of his kingdom. Or he might at least have lived out his final years under the kind care of his youngest daughter.

Finally, there is Macbeth. Fresh from victory in battle, Macbeth meets three witches who tell him he shall be "king hereafter." Enticed by the prospect of royal power, Macbeth entertains the idea of killing the reigning King Duncan and seizing the crown. Upon returning home, he thinks better of it, but Lady Macbeth dismisses his scruples and spurs him on to murder. After murdering the visiting Duncan and gaining the crown, Macbeth commits more murders to consolidate his position and suffers the mental consequences of his actions:

O, full of scorpions is my mind, dear wife!
(III.ii.41)

Lady Macbeth's mind is also in turmoil as she relives Duncan's murder while walking in her sleep and trying to wash imagined blood from her hands. Her doctor arrives, and Macbeth asks:

Canst thou not minister to a mind diseased,
Pluck from the memory a rooted sorrow,
Raze out the written troubles of the brain
And with some sweet oblivious antidote
Cleanse the stuff'd bosom of that perilous stuff
Which weighs upon the heart? (V.iii.50-55)

The doctor replies:

Therein the patient
Must minister to himself. (V.iii.56-57)

And Macbeth responds:

Throw physic to the dogs; I'll none of it. (V.iii.58)

He fails to understand that we must look after our own minds. No doctor can do it for us. Lady Macbeth commits suicide, and Macbeth is left to brood on the futility of his existence, finding life a tale:

...told by an idiot, full of sound and fury,
Signifying nothing. (V.v.29-31)

Macduff soon arrives with an avenging army to kill him. But it didn't have to be that way. There was a moment in which Macbeth could have heeded his better nature, curbed his lust for power, and overruled his wife. Had he done so, he might have gone on to live a long and happy life. And there was a moment in which Lady Macbeth might have paused, listened to her conscience, and dropped all thoughts of homicide. Had she done so, she might have enjoyed the

26

blessings of a peaceful mind, blessings no doctor can provide.

Othello, King Lear, Macbeth, and Lady Macbeth fail to guard their minds and are overcome by destructive emotions that cause enormous suffering. We risk falling into the same trap if we do not heed the advice of the eleventh century Tibetan Buddhist master, Geshe Langri Tangpa:

> *In my every action, I will watch my mind,*
> *And the moment destructive emotions arise,*
> *I will confront them strongly and avert them,*
> *Since they will hurt both me and others.*[18]

With vigilance, we can extinguish a spark of mental disturbance before it erupts into a raging housefire of negative emotion. But as the Buddha and Shakespeare both knew, if we fail to guard our minds, we open the door to terrible suffering for ourselves and others. Suffering is the subject of our next two chapters.

5

Suffering

SUFFERING IS AN INESCAPABLE part of
life. This is not what we want to hear, but
the Buddha's teaching on the truth of suffering (the first of his Four Noble Truths) is a
necessary first step on the path from suffering to
happiness and ultimate freedom. To take that
path, we must acknowledge suffering and recognize its many forms. The Buddha teaches that:

> Birth is suffering; aging is suffering; sickness is
> suffering; death is suffering; sorrow and lamenta-
> tion, pain, grief and despair are suffering; associa-
> tion with the loathed is suffering; dissociation
> from the loved is suffering; not to get what one
> wants is suffering.[19]

Even those of us fortunate enough to enjoy
health, prosperity, and security suffer from
stress, negative emotions, or, at the very least, a
vague sense of unease, together with the
knowledge that we and those we love will grow

old, get sick, and die. *Dukkha,* the Sanskrit word for suffering, means unease or dis-ease. It is one of the three marks or basic characteristics of existence taught by the Buddha. The others are impermanence (*anicca*) and egolessnes or not-self (*anatta*). We will get to them later.

Suffering is a truth unforgettably depicted in *Othello, King Lear,* and *Macbeth.* These characters endure mental anguish that is worse than any physical pain. But suffering is not confined to the central figures of high tragedy. Shakespeare's characters undergo many forms of suffering, and he makes us feel their pain. Consider these lines from *King John,* spoken by the Lady Constance after her son, Arthur, is taken prisoner by his usurping uncle, King John:

> *Grief fills the room up of my absent child,*
> *Lies in his bed, walks up and down with me,*
> *Puts on his pretty looks, repeats his words,*
> *Remembers me of all his gracious parts,*
> *Stuffs out his vacant garments with his form:*
> *Then have I reason to be fond of grief. (III.iv.95-100)*

We don't just observe grief in these lines. We sense what it feels like for the grief-stricken

Constance, who goes mad and dies. Shakespeare may have written *King John* soon after the death of his only son, Hamnet. Abraham Lincoln repeated the first two lines of this speech to an aide three months after his own son, Willie, died.[20]

Macbeth's nemesis, Macduff, endures an even greater loss when he learns that agents of Macbeth have murdered his wife and children. Advised to "dispute it like a man," he responds with an expression of grief:

> *I shall do so,*
> *But I must also feel it as a man.*
> *I cannot but remember such things were*
> *That were most precious to me. Did heaven look on*
> *And would not take their part?* (IV.iii.260-264)

Macduff understands that grief must be endured before healing can begin.

The woes endured by Othello, Lear, Macbeth, Lady Macbeth, the Lady Constance, and Macduff are all extreme examples of what Buddhists call the suffering of suffering or blatant suffering, which is entirely painful while it lasts.[21] The suffering of suffering also happens when multiple misfortunes befall us, "when sorrows come... not single spies, but in battalions," as Claudius says in *Hamlet*.

Disasters such as the loss of a child or a whole family would cause anyone to suffer. But we can create plenty of misery without such catastrophes by pursuing pleasures that lead to regret. *Sonnet 129* describes what happens when we allow our desires to get the better of us.

> *Th' expense of spirit in a waste of shame*
> *Is lust in action; and till action, lust*
> *Is perjured, murd'rous, bloody, full of blame,*
> *Savage, extreme, rude, cruel, not to trust,*
> *Enjoyed no sooner but despisèd straight,*
> *Past reason hunted; and, no sooner had*
> *Past reason hated as a swallowed bait*
> *On purpose laid to make the taker mad...*
> *All this the world well knows; yet none knows well*
> *To shun the heaven that leads men to this hell.*

The speaker tells us that until he acts on them, his cravings are beyond all reason. There may be bliss in the instant of gratification, but woe follows. He says in the closing couplet that we know what will happen but don't know how to stop ourselves. As the eighth-century Indian

Buddhist master Shantideva wrote of sentient beings:

> *Though longing to be rid of suffering,*
> *They rush headlong towards suffering itself.*
> *Although longing to be happy, in their ignorance*
> *They destroy their own well-being, as if it were*
> *their worst enemy.*[22]

Pleasurable experiences (sex, food, drugs, alcohol, power, and possessions) are transitory. When we pursue and cling to them out of our longing to be happy and avoid suffering, we only bring on what Buddhists call the suffering of change. The suffering of change is the pain of losing or knowing we will lose what we desire.[23] Or in the case of Shakespeare's sonnet, it is the pain of knowing that the instant of pleasure obtained at "the expense of spirit" has vanished and left only "a waste of shame."

Another form of suffering found in Shakespeare is sadness or melancholy, which is expressed by Hamlet when he says:

> *I have of late, but wherefore I know not, lost all my*
> *mirth, forgone all custom of exercises, and, indeed,*
> *it goes so heavily with my disposition that this*

goodly frame, the Earth, seems to me a sterile
promontory; this most excellent canopy, the air,
look you, this brave o'erhanging firmament, this
majestical roof, fretted with golden fire—why, it
appeareth nothing to me but a foul and pestilent
congregation of vapors. (II.ii.318-327)

Hamlet says he does not know why he finds the earth and the heavens unhealthy and suffocating. The merchant, Antonio, in *The Merchant of Venice* is another character who cannot account for his sadness. In the play's opening lines, he says.

In sooth I know not why I am so sad.
It wearies me, you say it wearies you.
But how I caught it, found it, or came by it,
What stuff 'tis made of . . . I am to learn. (I.i.1-4)

In the opening lines of the next scene, Portia adds to the melancholy atmosphere, saying:

By my troth, Nerissa, my little body is aweary of
this great world. (I.ii.1-2)

These speeches exemplify an undertone of sadness that we find throughout Shakespeare. Whatever the merriment, melancholy is rarely

33

far away. At the end of Shakespeare's comedies, there is usually at least one aggrieved or melancholy character, a Malvolio or a Jacques, who stands apart from the celebration to remind us that suffering continues under the happiest circumstances.

The sadness that underlies Shakespeare's works corresponds to what Buddhists call the all-pervasive suffering.[24] Because we fail to understand or address the causes of suffering, we find life unsatisfactory. The all-pervasive suffering can be like background noise. We may not be aware of it until it stops. For most of us, the all-pervasive suffering rarely stops.

6

The Causes of Suffering

T HE SECOND NOBLE TRUTH taught by
the Buddha is the truth of the causes of
suffering. The causes are attachment and
aversion arising from ignorance of the nature of
reality.[25] We are in a state of ignorance when we
fail to appreciate that everything is: (1) impermanent, (2) interdependent, and (3) made up of
parts that can be broken down into ever smaller
parts.

In our ignorance, we see permanence where
there is change, independence where there is interdependence, and singleness or solidity where
there is multiplicity. Thus deluded, we develop
attachments and aversions to things that do not
exist in the way we think, and we suffer. Crav-
ing, clinging, fear, disgust, anger, pride, self-ha-
tred, jealousy, and lust for power are also causes
of suffering, but all are forms of attachment or
aversion arising out of ignorance. They are the
negative emotions that will destroy us if we fail

to watch our minds and control them before
they control us.

We have seen these negative emotions at work
in *Othello, King Lear,* and *Macbeth.* Othello's jealousy, Lear's anger, and the Macbeths' lust for
power bring misery heaped on misery. Caught
in the grip of delusion, Othello kills Desdemona
and himself, Lear goes mad, Lady Macbeth goes
mad and kills herself, and Macbeth obtains a
"fruitless crown," only to end with his head on a
pike. All four fail to master their minds and, as
Shantideva says, "destroy their own well-being
as if it were their worst enemy."

Shakespeare wrote ten history plays about
kings of England, and a "fruitless crown" is at
the center of each of them. The crown is the chief
object of attachment, the prize for which characters are ready to kill and be killed. They may
scheme, wage battles, commit murders, and
bring on untold destruction, but if they obtain
the crown, they find that royal power is neither
indivisible, nor independent, nor lasting. For example:

- Henry VI sees his realm split apart as territo-
  ries in France are lost.

- Richard II and Henry VI are deposed and murdered.
- Richard III is killed in battle after allies desert him.
- King John, Henry IV, and Henry V get sick and die.

Shakespeare captures the futility of royal power in the *"hollow crown"* speech from *Richard II*. Shortly before he is deposed, Richard laments:

> *within the hollow crown*
> *That rounds the mortal temples of a king*
> *Keeps Death his court and there the antic sits,*
> *Scoffing his state and grinning at his pomp,*
> *Allowing him a breath, a little scene,*
> *To monarchize, be fear'd and kill with looks,*
> *Infusing him with self and vain conceit,*
> *As if this flesh which walls about our life,*
> *Were brass impregnable, and humour'd thus*
> *Comes at the last and with a little pin*
> *Bores through his castle wall, and farewell king!*
> *(III.ii.165-175)*

Shakespeare's hollow crown symbolizes the emptiness of power and position.

The crown brings little happiness, even to kings

who keep their thrones and die in their beds. In *Henry IV, Part 2*, Henry has insomnia. Lying awake, perhaps with a troubled conscience, he thinks of a sea-boy slumbering on a mast during a storm.

> *Canst thou, O partial sleep, give thy repose*
> *To the wet sea-boy in an hour so rude,*
> *And, in the calmest and most stillest night,*
> *With all appliances [expedients] and means to boot,*
> *Deny it to a king? Then, happy low, lie down.*
> *Uneasy lies the head that wears a crown. (III.i.26-31)*

Henry IV might well have trouble sleeping at night. By deposing Richard II and seizing his throne, he has set off a chain of events that will lead to the Wars of the Roses, the real *Game of Thrones*, with all their attendant slaughter. The hollow crown lures the ignorant into power plays that bring death and destruction for generations.

In exploring the causes of suffering, we have focused mainly on characters who bring misery to themselves and others by acting out of jealousy, anger, and lust for power. If we don't fall prey to such negative emotions, we will suffer less, but we will still suffer if we have worldly attachments and aversions. "Birth is suffering," teaches the Buddha.

> *When we are born, we cry that we are come*
> *To this great stage of fools. (IV.vi.200-201)*

says King Lear.

It may seem unfair that those who do little to bring suffering on themselves sometimes endure terrible misfortunes. But suffering is the common lot of all. Some believe it exhausts the consequences of negative actions from former lives. But we don't have to believe in rebirth or regard all suffering as punishment for past misdeeds. According to the Buddha, some causes of suffering, such as disease, natural disasters, and accidents, may be unrelated to our past actions.[26]

For Buddhists, the benefits of suffering go farther than exhausting the consequences of past misdeeds. Suffering can motivate us to follow a spiritual path, overcome attachment, aversion, and ignorance, and attain enlightenment. In the Buddhist scheme of things, rebirth as a human being is preferable to rebirth as a god, because gods do not suffer and therefore do not enjoy the benefits of suffering. Without those benefits, they must eventually take a lower rebirth. Only human beings can experience the benefits of suffering and attain enlightenment.

Shakespeare shows us suffering (the Buddha's First Noble Truth), and he shows us the causes of suffering (the Buddha's Second Noble Truth). The Buddha also taught that suffering ends when its causes are addressed (the Third Noble Truth). And he taught an eightfold path for addressing those causes (the Fourth Noble Truth). The eightfold path includes right understanding, intention, speech, action, livelihood, effort, mindfulness, and concentration. I will not try to use Shakespeare's words to illustrate each of these eight elements. Instead, I will focus on four immeasurable states of mind that grow out of the eightfold path.[27] We will explore them in our next two chapters.

7

Love, Compassion, Joy!

S ELFLESS DEDICATION to the well-being
of others helps reduce our suffering by
loosening attachment to the false notion of
a lasting, separate, and solid self. The greater
our concern for others, the less our attachment
to ourselves, and the less our attachment to ourselves, the greater our concern for others. As
Shantideva taught, suffering comes from
wanting pleasure for oneself; happiness
comes from wishing joy for others.[28] And the
Dalai Lama has said, "Our prime purpose in life
is to help others." So fundamental is this motivation that many Buddhist communities begin
their teachings and practices with *The Prayer of
the Four Immeasurables*:

> *May all sentient beings have happiness and the
> causes of happiness.*
> *May they be free from suffering and the causes of
> suffering.*

May they never be separated from the great happiness devoid of suffering.
And may they dwell in the great equanimity that is free from attachment and aversion.

The four immeasurable states of mind are:

- loving-kindness,
- compassion,
- sympathetic joy, and
- equanimity (the subject of our next chapter).

Loving-kindness is an attitude of unconditional benevolence, friendliness, or goodwill towards others. Buddhists begin their practice of loving-kindness by wishing happiness for themselves, because we must love ourselves before we can extend loving-kindness to others. They then wish happiness for someone dear to them, then for someone neutral, then for a difficult person, and finally for all beings unconditionally. Buddhists practice the other three immeasurables with the same all-embracing spirit. In this way, they cultivate a good heart, replacing selfish attachments with concern for their fellow beings.

None of Shakespeare's characters practice the

four immeasurables formally. We do not find them systematically training their minds to expand the scope of their altruistic motivation. And yet, some of Shakespeare's characters serve as good examples of loving-kindness, compassion, and sympathetic joy.

Loving-kindness

In expressing her love for Romeo, Juliet delivers lines that could describe the vast and inexhaustible quality of loving-kindness:

My bounty is as boundless as the sea.
My love as deep. The more I give to thee,
The more I have, for both are infinite. (II.ii.140-143)

But Juliet's loving-kindness is not as boundless as she thinks. It is limited because it is mixed with romantic attachment and focused on Romeo. She has the potential for loving-kindness that is truly boundless, but she has not had an opportunity to fully realize it. We must remember that Juliet is only thirteen years old.

The Shakespeare scholar, Harold C. Goddard, has written, "If Juliet is the morning star, Desdemona is the dawn."[29] If Juliet is incipient loving-kindness, Desdemona is loving-kindness itself. She gives her heart to Othello, but her kindness extends to others. When Lieutenant Cassio is dismissed by Othello for drunkenness, he asks her to help bring about a reconciliation. She welcomes an opportunity to promote the happiness of another and commits herself wholeheartedly to Cassio's cause, saying:

> If I do vow a friendship, I'll perform it
> To the last article. My lord shall never rest.
> (III.iii.23-24)

But the more she presses Cassio's suit, the more Othello resists. Her goodness has given the malevolent Iago the opening he needs to convince Othello that she is committing adultery with Cassio. As Othello falls into the grip of jealousy, he begins to abuse his wife verbally and physically. When her friend, Emilia, rightly suspects that she is a victim of slander, Desdemona doesn't believe it. Her nature is so far from doing harm that she can hardly conceive of harmfulness in others, but her benevolence extends even to her slanderer:

If any such there be, heaven pardon him.
(IV.ii.158)

After Othello suffocates his wife, Emilia asks:

O, who hath done this deed? (V.ii.151)

And Desdemona replies with her last words:

Nobody, I myself. Farewell.
Commend me to my kind lord. O, farewell.
(V.ii.152-153)

If I had to nominate one of Shakespeare's characters for sainthood, it would be Desdemona.

Compassion

Compassion is the natural response of love to the suffering of others. For Shakespeare, as for Buddhists, it is the heart that feels another's pain and longs to relieve it. As we saw earlier, *The Tempest* opens to the cries of mariners as their ship sinks in a storm conjured by the magician, Prospero. This sight brings a heartfelt expression of compassion from Prospero's young daughter, Miranda:

O, I have suffered
With those that I saw suffer! A brave vessel,
Who had, no doubt, some noble creature in her,
Dashed all to pieces. O, the cry did knock
Against my very heart! Poor souls, they perished.
Had I been any god of power, I would
Have sunk the sea within the earth or ere
It should the good ship so have swallowed, and
The fraughting [making up the freight] souls
within her. (I.ii.5-13)

In these lines, Shakespeare gives us the compassion of an innocent girl with little experience of the world. Miranda's compassion is a beautiful expression of innate human goodness.

Another tempest takes place in *King Lear*. Lear on the heath suffers from the storm without while enduring a greater storm of anguish within. But suffering awakens his compassion for the suffering of others. When he notices his fool shivering in the cold, he thinks not only of him but of all the others feeling the fury of the elements. His selfish heart opens, and he prays:

Poor naked wretches, wheresoe'er you are,
That bide the pelting of this pitiless storm,
How shall your houseless heads and unfed sides,

Your looped and windowed raggedness defend you
From seasons such as these? O, I have ta'en
Too little care of this. Take physic, pomp.
Expose thyself to feel what wretches feel,
That thou may'st shake the superflux to them
And show the heavens more just. (III.iv.28-36)

While Miranda's compassion is the compassion of innocence, Lear's is the compassion of experience. Through great suffering, he realizes that he has been blind to the plight of others. When his heart opens, he finds relief from his own distress, if only for a moment.

Like loving-kindness, compassion is boundless. The more compassion we feel for the suffering of others, the more our compassion grows. As compassion grows, it displaces attachment, aversion, and ignorance, thereby relieving our pain. Buddhists liken compassion to a wish-fulfilling jewel that cannot be exhausted, bringing benefits to the giver and receiver alike. Sogyal Rinpoche, the author of *The Tibetan Book of Living and Dying*, uses the following lines from *The Merchant of Venice* to illustrate the open and unconstrained nature of compassion:[30]

The quality of mercy is not strained.
It droppeth as the gentle rain from heaven
Upon the place beneath. It is twice blest:
It blesseth him that gives and him that
takes. (IV.i.168-171)

For Shakespeare, compassion is the spontaneous expression of an innocent child on seeing a shipwreck and the prayer of an old man whose selfish heart opens to the distress of others. It is a transcendent virtue, falling from heaven and raining blessings on the giver and receiver alike.

Sympathetic Joy

Sympathetic joy is unselfish joy at the goodness and good fortune of others. If compassion is the natural response of love to others' suffering, sympathetic joy is the natural response of love to their happiness. We rejoice in their virtues, attainments, wealth, and success, wishing them even greater happiness. As we rejoice in the happiness of others, our happiness grows. The opposite of sympathetic joy is envy, the resentment of another's good fortune. Envy reflects the false notion that happiness is a limited commodity, and that life is a zero-sum game in which one person's gain is another's loss.

Much Ado About Nothing opens on a note of sympathetic joy at the achievements of young Count Claudio as he returns with Signor Benedick from a military expedition. They gather at the home of Leonato, Governor of Messina. Hearing that Claudio's accomplishments have brought tears of happiness to his uncle, Leonato says:

> *There are no faces truer than those that are so washed.*
> *How much better is it to weep at joy than to joy at weeping! (I.i.26-29)*

With these words, Leonato defines a conflict at the heart of the play, the conflict between joy and envy.

The joy increases as Claudio seeks and wins the hand of Leonato's daughter, Hero. Hero, Claudio, and others of the party want to spread the joy to their best friends, Beatrice and Benedick, both self-professed bachelors and rivals in wit. They devise a plan to bring their friends "into a mountain of affection the one with the other." Male characters maneuver Benedick into overhearing a conversation about how much Beatrice loves him, and female characters maneuver Beatrice into eavesdropping on a conversation about Benedick's love for her. Their scheme succeeds, and Beatrice and Benedick become engaged, adding to the joyous atmosphere.

But Don John, an enemy of Claudio and a "plain dealing villain," is already plotting to ruin everything. Upon hearing of Claudio's good fortune, he says:

> *Any bar, any cross, any impediment will be med'cinable [curative] to me. I am sick in displeasure to him, and whatsoever comes athwart his affection ranges evenly with mine. (II.ii.4-7)*

Don John is one to joy at weeping. He devises a plot to convince Claudio that Hero entertains another lover on the night before their wedding, and Claudio falls for the deception. Infected by jealousy, he rejects and shames Hero before the assembled wedding guests. When Hero faints and appears to be dead, the officiating friar perceives her blamelessness and arranges to hide her away until her innocence is proven. Urged on by Beatrice, Benedick challenges Claudio to a duel, but after the bumbling constabulary exposes Don John's plot, they become friends again. The now repentant Claudio, still thinking Hero dead, agrees to marry her cousin, sight unseen. Then, posing as the cousin, Hero appears in a veil and says:

> *And when I lived, I was your other wife,*
> *And when you loved, you were my other husband. (V.iv.61-62)*

Beatrice and Benedick join them to make it a double wedding, and the play ends with a dance before the celebration of two marriages. Seven of Shakespeare's comedies end with the prospect of one or more weddings, and what is a wedding but a celebration of sympathetic joy at the happiness of others? What Shakespeare gives us at the end of his comedies is joy piled on joy. *The Tempest* ends with the betrothal [engagement] of one couple. *Much Ado About Nothing* and *The Two Gentlemen of Verona* end with the betrothal of two couples. *A Midsummer Night's Dream* and *Twelfth Night* end with the impending marriages of three couples. And *Love's Labour's Lost* and *As You Like It* each end with the betrothal of four couples.[31]

As audience members, we fully participate in the sympathetic joy depicted onstage. We celebrate the betrothal of the lovers. We rejoice that those thought to be dead are alive and restored to their loved ones. We delight in the virtues exemplified by the characters. And after the performance, we applaud the skill of the actors. We can even revel in the achievement of Shakespeare, who has been eliciting sympathetic joy from audiences on a vast scale for more than 400 years. For most of us, the feelings of sympathetic joy fade as we leave the theatre, but we would do well to retain and nurture them.

8

Equanimity

BUDDHIST EQUANIMITY has at least two aspects that we can relate to Shakespeare. The first involves freedom from attachment to gain, praise, fame, and pleasure and freedom from aversion to loss, blame, disrepute, and pain. Taken together, these are known as the eight worldly conditions. As forms of attachment and aversion arising from ignorance, all are sources of suffering.

The Buddha praises one who remains unwavering in the face of gain or loss, praise or blame, fame or disrepute, and pleasure or pain.[32] This kind of equanimity is the very quality that Hamlet admires in his friend, Horatio:

> *For thou hast been*
> *As one in suffering all that suffers nothing,*
> *A man that Fortune's buffets and rewards*
> *Hast ta'en with equal thanks; and blessed are those*
> *Whose blood and judgment are so well*

commeddled [commingled]
That they are not a pipe for Fortune's finger
To sound what stop she please. Give me that man
That is not passion's slave, and I will wear him
In my heart's core. (III.ii.69-78)

The composure that we find in Horatio reflects the Stoic philosophy familiar to Shakespeare from his reading of Seneca and other Romans. Such composure is achieved by overcoming attachment and aversion. It is no small achievement for a Buddhist or a Roman. But by itself, it lacks a second aspect of Buddhist equanimity, which is to regard all beings with an equal mind. It is this second aspect that makes equanimity one of the four immeasurables.

An equal mind is not an indifferent mind. We practice equanimity when we set aside our attachment to some and aversion for others and remember that all have inner goodness and want to be happy. With an all-embracing spirit, we wish them freedom from obstacles that impede their happiness and obscure their better natures. Like the other three immeasurables, equanimity is, in the words of the Buddha, "abundant, exalted, measureless."[33] It has an open heart as well as an untroubled mind.

In Shakespeare's plays, we find characters like Horatio who appear to be free of the eight worldly conditions. But we do not find characters who make it a point to regard all beings – friends, enemies, and everyone in between – equally. Nor do we, as audience members, look on all of Shakespeare's characters equally. Drama, by its nature, elicits attachment and aversion.

And yet, with Shakespeare's characters, our aversion is usually tempered because we come to know them so well.[34.] Out of his all-encompassing imagination, Shakespeare has created a great variety of multifaceted characters and given us a window into their innermost thoughts. In them, we see ourselves, or who we would like to be, or who we fear we could become, or who we might have become under different circumstances. When we experience *Hamlet*, we know what it is to be Hamlet and what it is to be Ophelia. We may even know what it is to be Gertrude or Claudius. In *Macbeth,* the title character is both a protagonist and a villain who tells us exactly what is going through his mind. We understand him, even as we are appalled by what he does. We see most of Shakespeare's characters as human beings like us trying, however misguidedly, to be happy and avoid suffering, and in this respect, they are the same as us.

Even Shakespeare's Richard II, who claims to rule by divine right, admits that he is essentially no different from anyone else when he says to his followers:

> *For you have but mistook me all this while.*
> *I live with bread like you, feel want,*
> *Taste grief, need friends. Subjected thus,*
> *How can you say to me I am a king? (III.ii.179-182)*

The conviction that others are essentially like us is given powerful expression by Shylock in *The Merchant of Venice*.

> *I am a Jew. Hath not a Jew eyes? Hath not a Jew hands, organs, dimensions, senses, affections, passions? Fed with the same food, hurt with the same weapons, subject to the same diseases, healed by the same means, warmed and cooled by the same winter and summer as a Christian is? If you prick us, do we not bleed? If you tickle us, do we not laugh? If you poison us, do we not die? (III.i.57-65)*

Yet these lines fall on deaf ears. Cruelly scorned and treated like a pariah, Shylock is driven to seek a gruesome revenge. In *The Merchant of Venice*, Shakespeare gives us an example of what can happen when we forget our common humanity and fail to treat others as we would have them treat us.

To the extent we see others as like us, we see them with an equal mind, whether they are kings or persecuted money lenders. Even Macbeth, or a real-life equivalent, wants to be happy as much as we do and should be included in our prayers. To pray for those who behave wickedly is not to excuse their wickedness. It is to wish them freedom from the delusions that cause it.

The Buddhist teacher, Pema Chödrön, describes equanimity as:

> *The vast mind that doesn't narrow reality into for and against, liking and disliking.*[35]

When prejudices arise, we can remember that the things we want and the things we don't want are without lasting, independent, or solid reality. And we can reflect that the people we like and the people we don't like have the same essential nature, whatever their delusions. With a heart that is "abundant, exalted, measureless," we wish them happiness, freedom from suffering, joy, and equanimity.

There is the equanimity that allows us to face the eight worldly conditions with calmness and composure, and there is the equanimity that enables us to regard others with an equal mind. Both depend on the extent to which we have overcome attachment and aversion and understood the nature of reality, which is impermanent as well as interdependent and made up of parts. Impermanence will be the subject of our next chapter.

9

Impermanence

THE BUDDHA TELLS A STORY about children building sandcastles by the side of a river. When one child kicks over another's sandcastle, there is a loud cry of protest, and the others set upon the offender. Then the children resume their play, each attached to their treasured creation and careful to defend it from any incursions. When evening approaches and it is time to go home, the children happily demolish the castles they had jealously protected only moments before.[36]

We forget impermanence and cling to things we know won't last. The only difference between the children and most of us is that our attachments do not usually go away with the onset of evening. We want to keep our sandcastles, whether they take the form of fame, power, position, relationships, money, or other possessions. But impermanence is a reality we cannot ignore for long, much as we might like to. As the Buddha taught:

Transient are all compounded things,
Subject to arise and vanish;
Having come into existence they pass away.[37]

Or, as Shakespeare wrote in Cymbeline:

Golden lads and girls all must,
As chimney-sweepers, come to dust. (IV.ii.335-
336)

Impermanence (*anicca*) is one of the three characteristics of existence taught by the Buddha. All phenomena are in a state of change. Some change in readily observable ways, like clouds and living beings. Others, like rocks and buildings, may appear permanent but are in continual change at the atomic level and will eventually disintegrate if not destroyed first.

In *Antony and Cleopatra*, Antony compares himself to clouds that change shape to resemble first a dragon, then a bear, and then a lion. He concludes by saying:

Here I am Antony,
Yet cannot hold this visible shape, (IV.xiv.18-19)

In Shakespeare's *Troilus and Cressida*, Cressida tells us more about impermanence than she intends when she vows to be true to Troilus:

If I be false or swerve a hair from truth,
When time is old and hath forgot itself,
When water drops have worn the stones of Troy
And blind oblivion swallowed cities up,
And mighty states characterless are grated
To dusty nothing, yet let memory,
From false to false, among false maids in love,
Upbraid my falsehood! (III.iii.187-193)

In vowing constancy, Cressida envisions a Troy that will last for eons into the future, until water drops have worn away its stones. Her vow notwithstanding, she transfers her affections to the Greek, Diomedes, after she is forced to join her father in the Greek camp. Audiences hearing Cressida's speech would perceive three kinds of impermanence. In her words, they would find the slow-acting change in which water drops wear away stones. Knowing Cressida will prove false, they would think of the impermanence of human affections. And knowing the story of the

Trojan War, they would think of the destruction that will come to Troy sooner than Cressida expects. While Cressida acknowledges slow-acting change, she has no idea how impermanent her world will prove to be.

Many of Shakespeare's sonnets are, in one way or another, about impermanence. In *Sonnet 64*, he describes how our seemingly solid world changes:

> When I have seen by Time's fell hand defaced
> The rich proud cost of outworn buried age;
> When sometime lofty towers I see down-razed
> And brass eternal slave to mortal rage;
> When I have seen the hungry ocean gain
> Advantage on the kingdom of the shore,
> And the firm soil win of the wat'ry main,
> Increasing store with loss and loss with store;
> When I have seen such interchange of state,
> Or state itself confounded to decay,
> Ruin hath taught me thus to ruminate,
> That Time will come and take my love away.
> This thought is as a death, which cannot choose
> But weep to have that which it fears to lose.

"Down-razed" towers would have been a common sight in Shakespeare's day, when the recently dissolved monastic establishments were torn down or quarried for their stone, and brass artifacts associated with the Roman Catholic faith went into the fire. Even the earth proves to be impermanent as the ocean washes it away and rearranges it. The speaker sadly reflects that if time can take away such solid-seeming phenomena, then it will surely take away his love. He can only weep to have that which he fears to lose.

In *Sonnet 73*, the speaker turns his attention to the impermanence of his own body. He makes us feel both the sweetness of life and the certainty of its passing:

> *That time of year thou mayst in me behold*
> *When yellow leaves, or none, or few, do hang*
> *Upon those boughs which shake against the cold,*
> *Bare ruined choirs where late the sweet birds sang.*
> *In me thou see'st the twilight of such day*
> *As after sunset fadeth in the west,*
> *Which by and by black night doth take away,*
> *Death's second self, that seals up all in rest.*
> *In me thou see'st the glowing of such fire*
> *That on the ashes of his youth doth lie,*
> *As the death-bed whereon it must expire,*
> *Consumed with that which it was nourished by.*

This thou perceiv'st, which makes thy love more strong,
To love that well which thou must leave ere long.

In the opening line, the speaker identifies with life at its lowest ebb and at its most precious. The tone is elegiac, but the images of decline are highly evocative: yellow leaves, bare ruined choirs, twilight fading into night, and the glow of a dying fire.

The final couplet drives home the point that imminent loss makes love stronger, and our response should be to love well. This response contrasts with the final couplet of *Sonnet 64*, where the response is to weep. In *Sonnet 64*, impermanence leads only to suffering, but in *Sonnet 73*, it also leads to love.

We love well when we embrace love and change in the same instant, recognizing that they are inseparable, and that change is a source of joy as well as sorrow. It will take our love away, but it brought our love to us in the first place. Without impermanence, nothing could change, grow, or live. To paraphrase the Zen master, Shunryu Suzuki, when we realize the truth of impermanence and accept it with equanimity, we will be beyond suffering.[38]

Like the children with their sandcastles, we grasp onto people and things as though they were permanent, but as the Buddha teaches, "All that is subject to arising is subject to cessation."[39] We can come to terms with the truth of impermanence, or we can argue with reality. Shakespeare shows us impermanence in many forms and provides a glimpse of the reconciliation to be found in acceptance of change. To realize impermanence is to remember that earthly existence is precious and fleeting.

In considering impermanence, we have also been considering mortality. We will have more to say about mortality in our next chapter.

10

Mortality

D EATH IS IMPERMANENCE as it affects the worldly existence of living beings. It happens when the conditions necessary for life are no longer present. In the words of the Buddha:

This existence of ours is as transient as autumn clouds.
To watch the birth and death of beings is like looking at the movement of a dance.
A lifetime is like a flash of lightning in the sky,
Rushing by, like a torrent down a steep mountain.[40]

And in the words of Hamlet:

Man's life's no more than to say 'one.' (V.ii.74)

The reality of death was more immediate for the contemporaries of the Buddha and of Shakespeare than it is for most of us today. In Shakespeare's London, the average life expectancy was 35 years. The bubonic plague swept the city four times during Shakespeare's lifetime. And for those who escaped the plague, there were epidemics of smallpox, typhus, and malaria, not to mention syphilis, which was widespread, lethal, and possibly the cause of Shakespeare's own death.[41] And then there were the gruesome public executions, and the decomposing heads of "traitors" displayed on London Bridge. Londoners confronted death and the horror of death every day. It wasn't any better for Shakespeare's characters. In his plays, no fewer than seventy-four die onstage: thirty by stabbing, five by beheading, seven by poisoning, and thirty-two by other means. Another eighty-one die offstage.[42]

Remembrance of death can turn the mind away from worldly pursuits and toward spiritual practice. Shortly before he died, the Buddha said:

> *Of all footprints*
> *That of the elephant is supreme;*
> *Of all mindfulness meditations*
> *That on death is supreme.*[43]

Death is the most powerful motivation for spiritual practice, and meditation on death is the supreme meditation. Perhaps no one expressed these teachings better than Tibet's great yogi and poet, Milarepa, who wrote:

> *In horror of death, I took to the mountains—*
> *Again and again I meditated on the uncertainty of the hour of death,*
> *Capturing the fortress of the deathless unending nature of mind.*
> *Now all fear of death is over and done.*[44]

There are no Milarepas in Shakespeare. Although many of Shakespeare's characters confront death, none attain Milarepa's realization. But some progress spiritually as they come to terms with death. Such a character is Hamlet.

Hamlet returns from school for his father's funeral to find that his uncle, Claudius, has seized the throne and married his mother. His mother and Claudius strongly discourage him from going back to school, and then the ghost of his father appears, tells how Claudius killed him, and urges his son to "Revenge his foul and most unnatural murder." As Hamlet considers what to do, he finds that Claudius is using his friends, and even his girlfriend, Ophelia, to spy on him.

Little wonder that Hamlet considers suicide in the opening lines of his famous soliloquy:

> *To be or not to be — that is the question:*
> *Whether 'tis nobler in the mind to suffer*
> *The slings and arrows of outrageous fortune,*
> *Or to take arms against a sea of troubles*
> *And, by opposing, end them. (III.i.56-60)*

The Vietnamese Buddhist master, Thich Nhat Hanh, has used Hamlet's "to be or not to be" to explain, by contrast, his own idea of inter-being. For Thich Nhat Hanh, "to be or not to be" is not the question because nothing can just be or not be. It can only inter-be. That is, phenomena cannot exist in isolation. They can only evolve in dependence upon countless causes and conditions. For example, we are a continuation of our parents and of all else that has influenced our present form of existence. As our parents continue in us, we will continue in what comes after. So, phenomena evolve endlessly.[45] The Greek philosopher, Heraclitus, made the same point when he said, "Everything flows, and nothing stays."[46] Or as he is also reported to have said, "Nothing is, everything is becoming."

Having accepted that reality is more than a matter of being or not being, we might look at another passage from the same soliloquy:

> *To die, to sleep—*
> *To sleep, perchance to dream. Ay, there's the rub,*
> *For in that sleep of death what dreams may come,*
> *When we have shuffled off this mortal coil [strife],*
> *Must give us pause. (III.i.72-76)*

In this passage, Hamlet reconsiders what he has just said about "to be or not to be." He thinks better of the proposition that he can, by the act of suicide, flip a switch from being to non-being. Hamlet abandons thoughts of suicide, but only because he fears death could bring a scarier form of being. He still thinks in terms of being and non-being. But the soliloquy does not contain Hamlet's last words about death.

Later in the play, Hamlet and Horatio visit a graveyard and engage in a contest of wit with a joking gravedigger. Hamlet seems at home among the bones as he holds the skull of Yorick, a jester well known to him from childhood, and addresses it thus:

Now get you to my lady's chamber, and tell her,
let her paint an inch thick, to this favor she must
come. Make her laugh at that. (V.i.199-202)

From contemplating the transience of physical
beauty, he turns to the transience of worldly
power:

Imperious Caesar, dead and turned to clay,
Might stop a hole to keep the wind away.
O, that that earth which kept the world in awe
Should patch a wall t' expel the win-
ter's flaw [blast]! (V.1.220-223)

Hamlet's contemplations at the bone-strewn
graveside call to mind Buddhist practitioners
who go to charnel grounds to meditate on death.
His mind has grown spacious enough to look at
life and death with apparent equanimity.

In the next scene, Hamlet prepares for a fenc-
ing match with Laertes before the court. Sus-
pecting, rightly, that there is a plot against Hamlet's life, Horatio says, "If your mind dislike anything obey it," and offers to cancel the match on
Hamlet's behalf. Hamlet replies:

Not a whit. We defy augury. There is a special
providence in the fall of a sparrow. If it be
now, 'tis not to come; if it be not to come, it will be
now; if it be not now, yet it will come. The readi-
ness is all. Since no man of aught he leaves knows,
what is 't to leave betimes? Let be. (V.ii.233-238)

"Readiness" implies a process in which causes
and conditions must unfold in a certain way before something can happen. The timing of a
sparrow's fall and the timing of a man's death
are determined by an ongoing interplay of factors. Hamlet's view now appears more con-
sistent with Thich Nhat Hanh's view that living
and dying are subject to inter-being.

While Hamlet's speech may be used to illustrate Buddhist teaching, it is grounded in Christian scripture. "Providence in the fall of a sparrow" alludes to the following words from the
Gospel of Matthew:

Are not two sparrows sold for a farthing, and
one of them shall not fall on the ground without
your Father? (Matthew 10:29)

The Christian idea of providence or divine care,
whether for the fall of a sparrow or the death of

a man, would have been a source of consolation for Shakespeare's contemporaries and, by extension, for Hamlet. Hamlet's equanimity in the face of death may also reflect the Stoicism that he praises in Horatio.

Facing the possibility of death, Hamlet can now say, "what is't to leave betimes? Let be." The timing of his death seems a matter of indifference. "Let be" expresses a surrender of attachment and aversion. Hamlet appears at peace with life and death and content to let causes and conditions unfold as they may. Of Shakespeare's characters, Hamlet may exhibit the most spacious mind. He may not realize its vast potential, but over the course of the play, he travels a long journey from "to be or not to be" to "let be." Still, Hamlet is neither a saint nor a buddha, at least not a fully realized one. His equanimity can give way to passion, as we see in the final scene when he kills Laertes and Claudius.

Like Hamlet and Milarepa, we know that we will die, but few of us act as if we believed it. We are caught in the illusion of a single, separate, and lasting *me.* Illusion is the subject of our next chapter.

11

Illusion

F OR THE BUDDHA, the world we encounter is without inherent reality. In the *Diamond Sutra*, he describes the appearances of this world as "a flickering lamp, a phantom, and a dream."[47]

And in *the King of Samadhis Sutra,* he says:

> *In the night the reflection of the moon*
> *Appears on clear, undisturbed water,*
> *But it is empty of a moon and there is nothing to grasp.*
> *Know that all phenomena are like that.*[48]

The Buddha sought, through his teachings, to make his followers aware of the illusory nature of everyday reality. He is also said to have conjured magical illusions when they served his purposes. Accounts of the Buddha's life tell of Queen Khema, the proud and beautiful consort of King Bimbisara. One day, Khema noticed a crowd gathered around the Buddha and went to hear his teaching. Seeing the Queen, the Buddha caused an image of a young and stunningly attractive girl to appear behind him, slowly waving a large fan. As he taught, she gradually became a mature woman, then middle-aged, then older with gray hair and wrinkles, and then an ugly crone. Finally, the image fell dead to the ground. Queen Khema, moved by this demonstration, gave up her position and followed the Buddha as a nun.[49]

Shakespeare was not a conjuror of magical displays, but he was a supremely gifted creator of theatrical illusions. These lines from *A Midsummer Night's Dream* could be read as a profession of his craft:

> *And as imagination bodies forth*
> *The forms of things unknown, the poet's pen*
> *Turns them to shapes and gives to airy nothing*
> *A local habitation and a name. (V.i.15-18)*

Out of "airy nothing," Shakespeare creates imaginary worlds inhabited by all sorts of illusions. Ghosts appear and disappear in *Hamlet, Macbeth, Julius Caesar, Richard III,* and *Cymbeline.* In *Macbeth,* the weird sisters disappear like bubbles in water. And as he goes to murder Duncan, Macbeth wonders if the spectral dagger that appears before him could be a hallucination:

> *Art thou not, fatal vision, sensible*
> *To feeling as to sight? Or art thou but*
> *A dagger of the mind, a false creation*
> *Proceeding from the heat-oppressèd brain?*
> *(II.i.47-50)*

Not all of Shakespeare's illusions are ghosts or products of a fevered brain. More often, they involve disguises and other man-made deceptions. Shakespeare had his bag of theatrical tricks and used them repeatedly.

- Twins are mistaken for each other (*The Comedy of Errors* and *Twelfth Night*).
- Women disguise themselves as men (*Two Gentlemen of Verona, As You Like It, Twelfth Night, The Merchant of Venice,* and *Cymbeline*).
- Men disguise themselves as women (*The Taming of the Shrew* and *The Merry Wives of Windsor*).
- Rulers disguise themselves as subjects (*Henry V* and *Measure for Measure*).

- Characters thought to be dead turn out to be alive (*All's Well that Ends Well, Cymbeline, Measure for Measure, Much Ado About Nothing, Pericles, The Tempest, Twelfth Night,* and *The Winter's Tale*).
- Men who think they are sleeping with an object of their illicit lust are sleeping with a rightful spouse (*All's Well That Ends Well* and *Measure for Measure*).

With his bag of tricks, Shakespeare shows how we lose ourselves in illusion and live under a multitude of false impressions. What the characters in Shakespeare's plays think they see often turns out to be man-made illusion. But in *The Tempest,* Shakespeare gives us more than supernatural, imagined, or man-made illusions. After conjuring and dissolving a masque of spirits, Prospero delivers these lines:

> *And like the baseless fabric of this vision,*
> *The cloud-capped towers, the gorgeous palaces,*
> *The solemn temples, the great globe itself,*
> *Yea, all which it inherit, shall dissolve,*
> *And, like this insubstantial pageant faded,*
> *Leave not a rack [wisp] behind. We are such stuff*
> *As dreams are made on, and our little life*
> *Is rounded with a sleep. (IV.i.165-175)*

Prospero is not talking only about magic or hallucinations. He tells us that material phenomena, like towers, palaces, temples, the globe itself, and all that will come after, are no more real than the baseless fabric of the vision he has just dissolved. And he is not only saying that buildings and the globe lack inherent reality. He tells us that "*we*" are also "such stuff as dreams are made on." The Buddha makes the same point when he likens our selves and all that we encounter to "a phantom and a dream."

The Buddha is not saying the self and material phenomena have no existence at all. That would be an assertion of nihilism, and the Buddha was not a nihilist any more than Shakespeare was a nihilist. He is saying that the self and phenomena appear but lack inherent existence because they are impermanent rather than lasting, interdependent rather than independent, and multiple rather than solid or single. And when Buddhists speak of phenomena as being empty, they are not talking about a void. While things may be empty of permanence, independence, and solidity, they are full of possibilities.

In *Measure for Measure*, Shakespeare echoes, point for point, Buddhist teaching on the nature of reality. In the play, the Duke of Vienna, disguised as a friar, visits a condemned man and counsels him to "be absolute for death" because the physical body he fears to lose is not lasting, independent, or single.

- It is not lasting because whatever we do to fly from death, we "runn'st toward him still." (III.i.13)
- It is not independent because we are at the mercy of influences that "this habitation" [the body] . . . "hourly afflict." (III.i.10-11)
- It is not single or solid because we are made up of "many a thousand grains that issue out of dust." (III.i.21-22)

The lack of permanence, independence, and solidity in material phenomena, including our bodies, is only part of the story. Our senses play a large part in determining what we take to be reality. Senses of sight, sound, smell, taste, and touch will vary from person to person and will vary far more widely from species to species. The world that you experience is not the world that your dog experiences. And what we perceive is never the thing itself, but signals (light waves, sound waves, etc.) interacting with sense organs and receptors in the brain and appearing in consciousness. Then there is an ever-changing array of mental predispositions that shape our perceptions, including prejudices, emotions, memories, expectations, and interests. In addition, there is a process that neuroscientists call sensory gating,[50] through which most sensory stimuli are filtered out before we ever become aware of them. We see things not as they are but as we are at a particular moment. We are indeed "such stuff as dreams are made on," with perceptions of reality varying from moment to moment and from person to person. Neither the subject of our perception (the perceiver) nor the objects (the perceived) are real in the way we think. The intrinsic existence that we attribute to them is an illusion.

The Buddha is said to have conjured magical illusions for the education of his followers, and Shakespeare created theatrical illusions for the entertainment of his audiences. But illusion was more than magic for the Buddha and more than theatrical invention for Shakespeare. Both understood that self and phenomena appear but do not exist as we tend to think. For the Buddha, this world is like a reflection of the moon in still water. And for Shakespeare, "The great globe itself, Yea, all which it inherit, shall dissolve."

12

Awakening

AWAKENINGS, LARGE OR SMALL, occur when illusions fall away. Most of Shakespeare's comedies end with small awakenings brought on by temporal revelations. With some of their illusions removed, the characters find their problems solved and their lives transformed for the better. *Twelfth Night* offers a good example.

Twins Viola and Sebastian (identical but for their genders) lose one another in a shipwreck on the coast of Illyria, and each thinks the other drowned. For protection, Viola takes on a male disguise and calls herself Cesario. She becomes a servant to Duke Orsino, with whom she secretly falls in love. But he loves the Lady Olivia and sends Viola/Cesario to deliver his amorous messages. But Olivia ignores the messages and falls in love with the messenger. Viola sums up the situation in four lines:

My master loves her dearly,
And I, poor monster, fond as much on him,
And she, mistaken, seems to dote on me.
What will become of this? (II.ii.34-36)

The play includes amusing subplots that I won't describe here. Suffice it to say that everything is in a terrible muddle until Viola's twin brother, Sebastian, shows up. Viola and Sebastian are thrilled to find one another alive, and the confusion ends when they disclose their true identities and genders to the amazement of the other characters. The play concludes in celebration, with Olivia betrothed to Sebastian and Viola betrothed to Orsino.

As exhilarating as these developments are, they have to do with temporal circumstances such as:

- who turns out to be alive after all,
- which twin is which,
- who turns out to be a woman in male disguise, and
- who will marry whom.

As audience members, we share in the joy these revelations bring, and we like to think of the characters living happily ever after. But this only happens in stories. In real life, human beings with attachments and aversions eventually suffer.

For Buddhists, awakening involves a greater revelation. It is no less than the revelation of the true nature of ourselves and the world around us. Such a revelation may come after years or lifetimes of dedicated practice.

The revelations experienced by the characters in *Twelfth Night* may be worldly, but for those inclined to see it, Shakespeare's words may sometimes point to something more. Consider the opening lines of the *Seven Ages of Man* soliloquy from *As You Like It*:

> *All the world's a stage,*
> *And all the men and women merely players;*
> *They have their exits and their entrances;*
> *And one man in his time plays many parts,*
> *His acts being seven ages. At first the infant,*
> *Mewling and puking in the nurse's arms;*
> *And then the whining school-boy, with his satchel*
> *And shining morning face, creeping like snail*
> *Unwillingly to school. (II.vii.146-154)*

If we meditate on these lines, we may begin to see our world as a stage on which the scenes and characters are constantly changing. The preoccupations that brought tears in childhood now bring a smile of amusement. We are no longer "the infant mewling and puking in the nurse's arms" or "the whining schoolboy with his satchel." We are now playing a different part. And years hence, when we are playing yet another part, we will probably have forgotten the preoccupations of today.[51]

What we think of today as our lasting, separate, and solid identity is only a role, one of many parts that we have played and will play. The people to whom we are close and those whom we dislike are themselves merely players. Over time, friends may become enemies, and enemies may become friends. We forget or never realize that we are much more than the parts we take so seriously.

But if we are not the parts we play, then who or what are we? Is there something that remains with us at every stage of life, from the "mewling and puking" babe of infancy to the "second childishness and mere oblivion" of extreme old age? Is there an aspect of our being that does not change? The Buddha points to such an aspect in the following words addressed to his community of monks:

> *Luminous, monks, is the mind, and it is defiled by incoming defilements.*
> *Luminous, monks, is the mind, and it is freed from incoming defilements.*[52]

We all have the potential to realize luminous mind, sometimes called buddha-nature, but luminous mind is obscured by the defilements of attachment and aversion arising from ignorance. Under their influence, we identify with whatever roles we are playing and mistakenly think they define us. Once freed from defilements, we would recognize our true nature, and luminous mind, which we share with all beings, would shine through.

The word, *luminous*, suggests a variation on Shakespeare's comparison of the world to a stage. We might say that all the world is a movie screen and all the men and women merely projections of light passing through film moving at 24 frames per second. The movie might depict any character or situation. We could be watching Audrey Hepburn in *Roman Holiday* or Boris

85

Karloff as Frankenstein's monster. But whatever appears on the screen, the light behind the film never changes. It remains luminous and pure from the first frame to the last.[53]

The movie projector analogy recalls the words of the Trappist monk, Thomas Merton:

Life is this simple: We are living in a world that is absolutely transparent, and God is shining through it all the time.[54]

If only we could recognize the luminosity or divine nature that shines through everything. We would see the projections for what they are and be free of the suffering that goes with playing a part. The movie of our life would then be stress-free and joyful.

Unhappily, for most of us attachments and aversions to the things of this world give rise to defilements that obscure our true nature and leave us trapped in illusion. Non-attachment is the subject of our next chapter.

13

Non-Attachment

IF THE THINGS OF THIS WORLD are no more lasting, independent, or solid than projections on a movie screen, then we would do well to stop clinging to them. Most of the suffering described in previous chapters resulted from some form of attachment or aversion. The more we let go of attachment and aversion the less we will suffer and the more we will enjoy the benefits of contentment and renunciation.

Contentment

A contented mind is carefree, calm, and composed. Such contentment comes with the first aspect of equanimity described in our chapter on equanimity. That aspect involves freedom from attachment to gain, praise, fame, and pleasure, and freedom from aversion to loss, blame, disrepute, and pain. The Buddha taught that there is no treasure like contentment, and we enjoy that treasure when untouched by these eight worldly conditions.

Shakespeare's pious Henry VI is an ineffectual king but a good example of contentment. In *Henry VI Part 3*, the Lancastrian Henry flees after losing a battle to his Yorkist rivals. He is apprehended, and when he claims to be the king, his captors ask to see his crown. He responds:

> *My crown is in my heart, not on my head;*
> *Not decked with diamonds and Indian stones,*
> *Nor to be seen. My crown is called content;*
> *A crown it is that seldom kings enjoy. (III.i.62-65)*

He is even content in prison, and when released, he thanks his jailor for making his imprisonment a pleasure. He is later re-arrested and confined in the Tower of London, where the future Richard III murders him. But Henry VI leaves us some of Shakespeare's best lines on contentment.

Duke Senior in *As You Like It* is a happier example of contentment. Deposed by his brother, he is content to live a simple life with his friends in the Forest of Arden, whatever the weather:

> *Here feel we but the penalty of Adam,*
> *The seasons' difference, as the icy fang*
> *And churlish chiding of the winter's wind,*
> *Which when it bites and blows upon my body*
> *Even till I shrink with cold, I smile and say*
> *"This is no flattery. These are counselors*
> *That feelingly persuade me what I am." (II.i.1-11)*

Duke Senior favors exposure to cold weather, the penalty of Adam, over exposure to the flattery of the court. At least the cold is an honest counselor that reminds him of his mortality. His words match the following advice given by the Buddha to the householder, Sigala, in *The Sigalovada Sutta*:

> *But he who does not regard cold or heat any more than a blade of grass and does his duties manfully, does not fall away from happiness.*

The Buddha goes on to advise Sigala to avoid false friends who flatter and pay lip service.[55] Following a path like the one recommended by the Buddha to Sigala, Duke Senior knows how to make the best of his situation:

Sweet are the uses of adversity,
Which, like the toad, ugly and venomous,
Wears yet a precious jewel in his head.
And this our life, exempt from public haunt,
Finds tongues in trees, books in the running
brooks,
Sermons in stones, and good in everything.
(II.i.12-17).

Duke Senior exemplifies contentment in nature and equanimity in the face of the eight worldly conditions.

In *A Midsummer Night's Dream*, we find our most amusing example of contentment. Nick Bottom the Weaver is one of six rude mechanicals [skilled laborers] who go into a forest to rehearse a play that they hope to present at court. Unknowingly, they have entered the realm of Oberon and Titania, King and Queen of the Fairies, who are fighting over a changeling boy that Titania has taken. With the help of the mischievous Puck, Oberon seeks to get even by anointing Titania's eyes with the juice of a flower which will cause her to love the next thing she sees.

As the amateur players begin their rehearsal, Puck changes Bottom's head into that of an ass. When they see him, the others flee, but Bottom, thinking nothing amiss, supposes they are playing a trick. To show them he is not afraid, he sings a song that awakens Titania. Seeing Bottom, she dotes on him, even with his ass's head. As he meets Titania's attendant fairies, Bottom responds to each with affable good humor. When Titania makes it clear that her services are at his command, he is ready for anything but would have been content with some hay and a nap. Deciding things have gone far enough, Oberon applies an antidote to Titania's eyes and has Puck give Bottom back his human head. When he awakens from sleep, Bottom says:

> *I have had a most rare vision. I have had a dream past the wit of man to say what dream it was. Man is but an ass if he go about to expound this dream. Methought I was—there is no man can tell what. Methought I was and methought I had—but man is but a patched fool if he will offer to say what methought I had. The eye of man hath not heard, the ear of man hath not seen, man's hand is not able to taste, his tongue to conceive, nor his heart to report what my dream was. I will get Peter Quince to write a ballad of this dream. It shall*

be called "Bottom's Dream" because it hath no
bottom. (IV.i.214-225)[56]

For me, Bottom exemplifies contentment under
extraordinary conditions. When his friends run
away, he walks up and down and sings a song.
When Titania professes her love, he plays along
happily. When he wakes, he is not at all dis-
mayed to have lost the services of a fairy queen
and her attendants but feels he has had the most
remarkable dream. When he is unable to recall
any details of the dream, he is fine with that too.
If his dream has no bottom, Bottom is content to
live with the mystery. He is happy where he is,
with what he has, and with what he can or cannot remember. If Bottom is a fool, he is a kind of
holy fool, open to whatever comes his way. He
is that rare character who appears to have no
lasting attachments or aversions.

Renunciation

In Buddhism and other spiritual traditions, non-
attachment may take the form of renunciation.
The Buddha's path to enlightenment began
when he left wife, child, palace, and royal

privileges in search of a refuge from old age, sickness, and death. Buddhists call this the Great Renunciation. During his search, he practiced extreme asceticism for six years and was reduced to skin and bones as he subsisted on a few grains of rice a day. Only after giving up this regimen and taking adequate nourishment did he attain enlightenment. In *The Dhammapada*, he warns against extreme self-denial:

> *But as a blade of grass held awkwardly*
> *May cut your hand,*
> *So renunciation may lead you into the dark.*[57]

The Buddha understood that asceticism can be a trap, with some ascetics more attached to their meager diets than gluttons to their lavish feasts. The Zen master, Shunryu Suzuki, reflected the Buddha's understanding when he said that:

> *Renunciation is not giving up things of this world but accepting that they go away.*[58]

In other words, renunciation is not about giving up things. Rather, it is about realizing that they are not lasting and letting go. But until we fully realize impermanence, letting go can be difficult, especially if we habitually occupy our minds with worldly concerns. Turning away from such concerns and toward a spiritual path can lead to disenchantment with old attachments.

We usually associate renunciation with those who become monastics or otherwise abandon the world to follow a religious life. But in Shakespeare, we find few religious renunciates. There is Henry VI, who relinquishes the exercise of royal power to others, preferring to:

> *lead a private life*
> *And in devotion spend my latter days,*
> *To sin's rebuke and my Creator's praise.*
> *(Henry.VI.3.vi.43-45)*

But Henry VI is a weak ruler who never goes so far as to give up his crown. In *As You Like It*, there is the usurping Duke Frederick, who undergoes a religious conversion, resigns his ill-gotten dukedom, and goes into a monastery. But Frederick is a minor character whose conversion is a plot device to help bring about the play's happy resolution. In *Measure for Measure* there is Isabella, who is a novice nun at the beginning of the play, although it is unclear at the end whether she will continue as a nun or marry.

But in Shakespeare, we find examples of what I will call secular renunciation. These limited renunciations are not associated with any religious tradition and not necessarily combined with any spiritual practice. They involve characters who become disenchanted with objects of attachment when they see their falsity and harmfulness. For example, Prince Hal in *Henry IV, Part 2*, renounces his association with unsavory companions, saying to Falstaff:

> *I know thee not, old man. Fall to thy prayers.*
> *How ill white hairs becomes a fool and jester.*
> *I have long dreamt of such a kind of man,*
> *So surfeit-swelled, so old, and so profane. . .*
> *(V.v.47-50)*

On becoming king, he awakens and repudiates the dissolute behavior in which he once took part. Giving up such behavior may not qualify Prince Hal as much of a renunciate, but at least it's a start.

Other characters outgrow in old age the attachments that once consumed them. Prospero in *The Tempest* was so obsessed with his books and the study of magic that he lost his dukedom to his wicked brother, Antonio. But after using his powers to regain his dukedom and arrange a happy marriage for his daughter, he renounces "rough magic," saying:

> I'll break my staff,
> Bury it certain fathoms in the earth,
> And deeper than did ever plummet sound
> I'll drown my book. (V.i.63-66)

He no longer wants or needs magic now that he is about to retire to Milan where, he says, "every third thought shall be my grave." Prospero is now ready to replace the pursuit of "rough magic" with preparation for death.

Another character who outgrows attachments is King Lear. After resigning his crown to his daughters, Lear discovers too late that he is still attached to the authority he has given away. Only after enormous suffering and a descent into madness is he finally ready to let go of power, position, and royal identity. He looks forward to life in prison as one of "god's spies" and says:

> Upon such sacrifices, my Cordelia,
> The gods themselves throw incense. (V.iii.22-23)

Sadly, Lear's renunciation of royal power cannot avert the play's final catastrophe.

Perhaps no character in Shakespeare is more thoroughly disenchanted with the world than Hamlet. He gives voice to bitter disillusionment in his opening soliloquy:

> How (weary) stale, flat, and unprofitable
> Seem to me all the uses of this world!
> Fie on 't, ah fie! 'Tis an unweeded garden
> That grows to seed. Things rank and gross in nature
> Possess it merely (I.ii.137-141)

But Hamlet's almost suicidal disgust with the rotten state of Denmark, while understandable, is not true renunciation. Hamlet is consumed by aversion to what his world has become, and his aversion is the flip side of attachment to what he thinks it should be. But as we observed in our chapter on mortality, Hamlet grows spiritually over the course of the play. By the penultimate scene, he is ready to let go of both aversion and attachment when he says, "Since no man of aught he leaves knows, what is't to leave betimes? Let be."

Since Hamlet knows nothing of what he leaves, he has no cause for attachment or aversion to the things of this world. He is ready to let be and accept whatever comes, including his own death. Letting be or letting go is the key to renunciation. Admittedly, my picture of Hamlet as a model of secular renunciation is contradicted by the violence of the final scene. But renunciation, like any state of mind, can be changeable, especially when not grounded in spiritual practice.

Secular renunciation has its limitations, but Shakespeare's secular renunciates have one thing in common with many Buddhist renunciates. Their renunciation, however limited, comes naturally because their readiness to let go is stronger than their desire to stay attached.

14

Non-Harming

A CCOUNTS OF the Buddha's life include
an episode in which he intervenes to stop
a war between the Shakyan and Kolyan
states. Arriving at the river separating them, the
Buddha finds the opposing forces drawn up and
ready to fight. None can say why war is necessary, but the two sides have exchanged insults,
and all agree honor demands a battle. The Buddha learns from local farmers that the cause of
the conflict is a shortage of water for irrigation.
He then asks the warriors if blood is not more
precious than water. The opposing armies listen
as the Buddha tells stories and gives teachings.
At last, they make peace. Not only is a bloody
battle averted, but 250 men from each side join
the Buddha's community of monks.[59]

In averting death and destruction, the Buddha
promotes the principle of ahimsa or non-harming, which is central to Buddhist ethics. "If you
can't help, at least don't harm," teaches the

Dalai Lama. Monastics and laypeople alike vow never intentionally to kill a sentient being. In Buddhist ethics, abstention from killing is the first of five precepts, the others being abstention from stealing, lying or hurtful speech, sexual misconduct, and intoxicants. We can harm others and ourselves by intentionally engaging in any of these behaviors.

This chapter will focus on harm in the form of violence and killing. Buddhists vow not to kill because they realize that others value their lives as much as we value ours. As the Buddha says in the Dhammapada:

> *All beings tremble before violence.*
> *All fear death.*
> *All love life.*
> *See yourself in others.*
> *Then whom can you hurt?*
> *What harm can you do?*[60]

By contrast, Shakespeare often seems to give us the very opposite of non-harming. *Romeo and Juliet* opens with a street brawl, and its plot turns on two deadly sword fights. In *Julius Caesar*, mobs roam the streets and kill indiscriminately. Macbeth, Richard III, and Claudius murder their way to royal power. And *King Lear, Macbeth, Hamlet, and Henry IV Part 1* each feature a dual to the death. And then there are the wars. Thomas Hardy wrote that "War makes rattling good history, but peace is poor reading."[61] Shakespeare was in the business of writing rattling good histories, and his plays feature no fewer than 16 battles. We could go on for pages listing examples of violence in Shakespeare. But where we find violence, we find the consequences of violence, and Shakespeare's portrayal of those consequences makes a powerful case for non-violence.

Of all Shakespeare's plays, *Henry V* is best known for the patriotic glorification of war, especially in Henry's stirring St. Crispin's Day speech. But a common soldier named Williams delivers the play's truest insights about war:

> *But if the cause be not good, the King himself hath a heavy reckoning to make, when all those legs and arms and heads, chopped off in a battle, shall join together at the latter day, and cry all "We died at such a place," some swearing, some crying for a surgeon, some upon their wives left poor behind them, some upon the debts they owe, some upon their children rawly [immaturely] left. I am afeard*

there are few die well that die in a battle, for how can they charitably dispose of anything when blood is their argument? Now, if these men do not die well, it will be a black matter for the king that led them to it, who to disobey were against all proportion of subjection. (IV.i.138-151)

King Henry, who is visiting his men in disguise on the eve of battle, dismisses these words. He says the King is no more responsible for a soldier killed in action than a father for a son who miscarries on an errand. But this is a weak argument. Sending someone on an errand and sending them into deadly combat are different matters altogether. Shakespeare allows Henry to appear to win the argument because he can't very well do otherwise, but he gives Williams the better case.

Shakespeare's plays contain vivid descriptions of the consequences of war. Among the most horrifying is this passage from *Henry V*, in which Henry describes the atrocities that will ensue if the citizens of Harfleur do not surrender their town:

If not, why in a moment look to see
The blind and bloody soldier with foul hand

Desire the locks of your shrill-shrieking daughters,
Your fathers taken by the silver beards
And their most reverend heads dashed to the walls,
Your naked infants spitted upon pikes
Whiles the mad mothers with their howls confused
Do break the clouds, as did the wives of Jewry
At Herod's bloody-hunting slaughtermen.
(III.iii.33-40)

The case for non-violence takes a lighter turn in *Henry IV Part 1*. Sir John Falstaff enlists to aid the King in putting down a rebellion, although he is more interested in profiting from the war and has no stomach for fighting. When reminded by Prince Hal that he "owes God a death," he responds with the following:

'Tis not due yet; I would be loath to pay him before his day. What need I be so forward with him that calls not on me? Well, 'tis no matter; honour pricks me on. Yea, but how if honour prick me off when I come on? how then? Can honour set to a leg? no: or an arm? no: or take away the grief of a wound? no. Honour hath no skill in surgery, then? no. What is honour? a word...What is in that word honour? What is that honour? air. A trim reckoning! Who hath it? he that died o' Wednesday. Doth he feel it? no. Doth he hear it?

no. 'Tis insensible, then. Yea,to the dead. But will
it not live with the living? no. Why? detraction
will not suffer it. Therefore I'll none of it. Honour
is a mere scutcheon [painted shield]: and so ends
my catechism. (V.ii.128-142)

Depending on your point of view, Falstaff is a
shameless coward or the sanest person on the
battlefield. Either way, his intentions have nothing to do with non-harming and everything to
do with saving his skin. And at the very least,
the old reprobate is guilty of causing harm
through drunkenness, lying, stealing, and sexual
misconduct. Still, Falstaff offers a human coun-
terpoint to the scenes of deadly combat and
memorably derides notions of "honour" that are
sometimes misused to promote violence.

In the late romances, *The Tempest, The Winter's
Tale, and Cymbeline,* Shakespeare does more than
show violence and its consequences. Each play
ends with the establishment of a new order
based on the peaceful resolution of old conflicts.
In the final scene of *Cymbeline,* Britain has defeated an invading army sent to force payment
of tribute to Rome. But rather than press his ad-
vantage, the British ruler, Cymbeline, seeks to

establish a lasting peace by pardoning the Roman general and agreeing to pay the tribute:

> *Publish we this peace*
> *To all our subjects. Set we forward. Let*
> *A Roman and a British ensign wave*
> *Friendly together. (V.v.580-582)*

Where war and peace are concerned, it is impossible to attribute a single point of view to Shakespeare. He was in the business of staging "rattling good histories." But the consequences of violence and the advantages of non-violence are well represented in his plays.

Because we are all interconnected, any harm we do, whether by violence, stealing, hurtful speech, sexual misconduct, or drunkenness, leads to more negative consequences than we can imagine. Interdependence is the subject of our next chapter.

15

Interdependence

W HEN CORDELIA CAN SAY nothing to outdo her sisters' false expressions of love, King Lear angrily warns, "Nothing will come of nothing." Without realizing it, he is saying something quite true, because nothing ever comes of nothing. All phenomena appear and disappear within a web of interconnected causes and conditions. Buddhist teachings on this subject can be involved, but the Buddha explains interdependence essentially in four lines:

> *When this is that is.*
> *From the arising of this comes the arising of that.*
> *When this isn't that isn't.*
> *From the cessation of this comes the cessation of that.*[62]

In our chapter on the causes and benefits of suffering, we identified interdependence as one of three reasons why phenomena do not exist as we tend to think. And in our chapter on mortality, we saw how Thich Nhat Hanh uses Hamlet's "to be or not to be" to explain, by contrast, interdependence or inter-being. For him, "to be or not to be" is not the question because reality is not a matter of fixed states like being or not being. Rather, it is a matter of inter-being, a continual unfolding of causes and conditions.

In another explanation of inter-being, Thich Nhat Hanh uses the example of a sheet of paper. He says that in the paper, we should see the rain clouds and the sunshine that provided the right conditions for the forest that supplied the wood used to make the paper. We could also see the logger who cut the tree and the food he ate. We could go on forever describing the innumerable causes and conditions that come together in just one sheet of paper. We should not forget to add ourselves to the picture, because without our presence, there would be no perception of the paper. [63] And as we noted in our chapter on illusion, our perception depends on our sensory capacities and a changing mix of mental inclinations, which in turn depend on an incalculable multitude of factors.

When Romeo and Juliet first see one another, their sensory capacities and mental inclinations cause them to fall madly in love. Like other lovers, they would like to exist only for each other, undisturbed by the world around them. But this would be difficult under the best conditions, and Romeo and Juliet face major obstacles. They live in a society in which girls are married at a very young age to suitors chosen by their fathers. And their feuding families, the Capulets and Montagues, are caught in a deadly cycle of violence and revenge. These and other factors give rise to a host of causes and conditions that join against them. The prologue to the play describes the lovers as "star-crossed," but the circumstances that bring about their tragedy unfold here on earth. The tragedy would not have happened:

- If hot weather had not stirred the hatreds of the Capulet and Montague households.
- If their brawl had not led to an edict against further disturbances.
- If the Capulets had not given a party.
- If their serving-man had not shown Romeo the guest list.
- If Romeo had not gone to the party.
- If Tybalt had not recognized him.

- If Romeo and Juliet had not met, fallen in love, and exchanged vows.
- If Tybalt had not provoked a fight and killed Mercutio.
- If Romeo had not killed Tybalt.
- If Juliet's father had not insisted she marry Paris.
- If Friar Lawrence's messenger had not been detained due to a plague, etc.

These are just a few of the countless causes and conditions that bring about the tragedy. But the process does not end when Romeo and Juliet breathe their last in the tomb of the Capulets. In the final scene, Shakespeare brings the Capulets and Montagues together in grief to honor their children and end their deadly feud. These events will lead to further and, we hope, happier developments.

The interdependence that we see in *Romeo and Juliet* does not unfold by linear progression. It is not a matter of A causes B which in turn causes C, and so on until we reach an end point. Rather, it is a matter of innumerable factors acting on each other simultaneously and continuously with no end point.

Whatever Shakespeare may have thought about the power of the stars to determine destiny, his plays show how everything proceeds from an ongoing interplay of causes and conditions. We can call this interplay interdependence, interconnection, or inter-being.

Shakespeare takes us only so far, however. We cannot use his works to illustrate all Buddhist teachings on interdependence. For many Buddhists, twelve links of dependent origination[64] drive a painful cycle of birth, death, and rebirth that will continue for eons until we attain enlightenment.

Whether or not we believe in a cycle of birth, death, and rebirth driven by twelve links of dependent origination, we are interdependent beings. An unimaginable number of causes and conditions had to come together exactly as they did to bring about the transient manifestations that we call ourselves. And everything we do or do not do, down to the smallest action or inaction, will affect our future, the futures of others, and all that comes after. If everything is interdependent, then we cannot be too careful about our actions.

Padmasambhava, the venerated eighth-century master who helped establish Buddhism in Tibet, said:

> *Although my view is higher than the sky,*
> *My respect for the cause and effect of actions is as*
> *fine as grains of flour.*[65]

Actions and consequences will be considered in our next chapter.

16

Actions and Consequences

THE INTENTION BEHIND every action, large or small, contributes to our future happiness or unhappiness. The Buddha warns:

> But as dust thrown against the wind,
> Mischief is blown back in the face
> Of the fool who wrongs the pure and harmless.[66]

This teaching is associated with *karma*, a Sanskrit word that refers to the cause and effect of actions. But Buddhist teachings on karma can be challenging, and they involve rebirth, which was not a common or accepted belief in Shakespeare's England.[67] So, we can't say that Shakespeare believed in karma. But his plays do illustrate three central tenets of karma:

- Actions bring consequences.
- The intentions behind the actions determine the consequences.

- Good intentions bring good consequences,
  and bad intentions bring bad consequences.

As the Buddha says in *The Dhammapada*:

It is better to do nothing
Than to do what is wrong,
For whatever you do you do to yourself.[68]

Such advice is not unique to Buddhism. According to St. Paul, "As ye sow so shall ye reap," or in modern parlance, "what goes around comes around."

Shakespeare often shows us that ill-intended actions bring bad consequences for the actor. Let's begin with *Richard III*. While seizing and securing the English crown, Richard commits eleven murders. In the end, despite all his machinations, Richard is killed in battle on Bosworth Field. To leave no doubt that ignominious death is the direct consequence of his actions, Shakespeare has the ghost of each victim appear to Richard on the eve of battle to recount the circumstances of their murder and bid him "despair and die."

We have seen the consequences that Macbeth and Lady Macbeth bring on themselves by their murderous actions. Before killing Duncan, Macbeth foresees them:

> But here, upon this bank and shoal of time,
> We'd jump the life to come. But in these cases
> We still have judgment here; that we but teach
> Bloody instructions, which, being taught, return
> To plague th' inventor. This even-handed justice
> Commends th' ingredients of our poisoned chalice
> To our own lips. (I.vii.8-12)

After committing the murder, Macbeth looks at his hands and sees that he will not be able to escape the consequences of what he has done:

> What hands are here! Ha, they pluck out mine eyes.
> Will all great Neptune's ocean wash this blood
> Clean from my hand? No, this my hand will rather
> The multitudinous seas incarnadine,
> Making the green one red. (II.ii.77-81)

Something similar happens to Claudius in Hamlet. After murdering his brother, seizing his kingdom, and marrying his queen, Claudius tries to pray for forgiveness but finds that his prayers ring hollow and will never bring absolution:

> *May one be pardoned and retain th' offense?*
> *In the corrupted currents of this world,*
> *Offense's gilded hand may shove by justice,*
> *And oft 'tis seen the wicked prize itself*
> *Buys out the law. But 'tis not so above:*
> *There is no shuffling; there the action lies*
> *In his true nature, and we ourselves compelled,*
> *Even to the teeth and forehead of our faults,*
> *To give in evidence. (III.iii.60-68)*

Richard III, Macbeth, and Claudius were not fated to be murderers. They each make a free choice to kill others to satisfy their lust for power, and each comes to a bad end. Before they are killed, we see them suffering the mental consequences of their actions. Richard is haunted by ghosts. Macbeth's mind is full of scorpions. And Claudius' soul is like a trapped bird "that struggling to be free art more engaged." For Buddhists, mental consequences matter most, and Shakespeare portrays them vividly.

We can easily accept that Richard III, Macbeth, and Claudius must suffer the consequences of their murderous actions, but in other instances, the unfolding of actions and consequences can seem harsh. Consider the Duke of Gloucester in *King Lear*. Although he has been a philanderer and begotten an illegitimate son, he has a kind heart. When he tries to relieve Lear's suffering, the illegitimate son, Edmund, betrays him to Lear's enemies. In one of Shakespeare's most painful scenes, Gloucester is tied to a chair, and his eyes are gouged out as punishment for his kindness. When Gloucester's legitimate son, Edgar, confronts the wicked Edmund at the end of the play, he says:

> *The gods are just, and of our pleasant vices*
> *Make instruments to plague us.*
> *The dark and vicious place where thee he got*
> *Cost him his eyes. (V.iii.204-207)*

In the pre-Christian Britain of *King Lear*, the consequences of misbehavior can be extreme. Gloucester finds nothing in the cosmic order but arbitrariness and cruelty when he says:

> *As flies to wanton boys are we to th' gods;*
> *They kill us for their sport. (IV.1.41-42)*

But physical and mental pain are the common lot of all, and suffering can bring benefits. As we have seen, for Hamlet, it brings the wisdom to look on life and death with apparent equanimity. For King Lear, it brings compassion for the "poor, naked wretches" in the storm. For Gloucester, it at least brings the patience to agree that:

> Men must endure
> Their going hence, even as their coming hither;
> Ripeness is all. (V.ii.8-10)

The greatest benefit suffering can bring is the motivation to follow a spiritual path, overcome attachment, aversion, and ignorance, and attain enlightenment.

We may take consolation in knowing that suffering can lead to wisdom, compassion, enlightenment, or at least patience. But what about characters who don't survive? Cordelia, Desdemona, Lady Macduff, and her children are brutally killed through no fault of their own. These innocents will have no opportunity for further growth in this life. We need to believe that they will find their transcendence in another. Although rebirth was not part of their established belief system, Shakespeare's contemporaries did believe in a hereafter. The ghost of Hamlet's father says that he is:

Doomed for a certain term to walk the night
And for the day confined to fast in fires
Till the foul crimes done in my days of nature
Are burnt and purged away. (I.v.15-18)

Actions and consequences in Shakespeare's plays are not always balanced, nor are they balanced over a single lifetime. So, Buddhists believe in rebirth, and Shakespeare's contemporaries believed in a hereafter, both trusting that bad actions will be "burnt and purged away" and that goodness will find its reward.

But not all who have done wrong are doomed to suffer the full consequences. Genuine remorse can mitigate the consequences of harmful actions. Remorse is the subject of our next chapter.

17

Remorse

REMORSE MEANS: (1) acknowledging an action, (2) recognizing its negative consequences, (3) doing what we can to repair and purify them, and (4) resolving never to repeat the action. Remorse differs from guilt and shame in that it condemns the deed, not the doer, the sin, not the sinner. Buddhists believe that we can atone for even the worst actions because our fundamental nature, sometimes called *buddha-nature*, remains unstained, however much it is obscured.[69] Wrong actions may be what we do, but they are never who we are.

In Buddhist lore, we find tales of fearsome beings who encounter the Dharma, come to regret their wickedness, and lead blessed lives. One of the worst is Angulimala, a bandit and murderer who wears a necklace of fingers taken from his 999 victims. The Buddha sets off to find Angulimala to stop the carnage and keep him from piling up more evil karma. Angulimala tries to make the Buddha his one-thousandth victim, but a magic spell keeps him at a distance. Unable to catch up to the Buddha, Angulimala yells, "Stop," but the Buddha tells the bandit that it is he who must stop his killing. One look into the Buddha's eyes is all it takes to change Angulimala's heart. Overcome by remorse, he learns the Dharma, follows the Buddha as a monk, serves others, and eventually attains nirvana. His story demonstrates that all beings have buddha-nature, however badly they may have acted.[70]

No characters in Shakespeare behave quite like Angulimala, but some behave badly enough. Consider King Leontes of Sicilia in *The Winter's Tale*. When he imagines that his wife, Hermione, has committed adultery with the visiting King Polixenes of Bohemia, Leontes behaves abominably. He imprisons Hermione, takes away her son, and tries to have the fleeing Polixenes poisoned. When Hermione gives birth to a girl, Leontes assumes it is Polixenes' child, threatens to have it burned, and orders it abandoned to the elements. Leontes refuses to relent, even when the Oracle of Apollo confirms Hermione's innocence. Only when his son dies because of his actions does Leontes recognize his mistake. When

Hermione swoons upon learning of the boy's death, Leontes thinks she is also dead, but she is alive and is secretly taken into the care of her friend, Paulina.

At the beginning of the play, before the king's attack of jealousy shatters their lives, Polixenes tells Hermione about his happy childhood days with Leontes:

> *We were as twinned lambs that did frisk i' th' sun*
> *And bleat the one at th' other. What we changed*
> *Was innocence for innocence. We knew not*
> *The doctrine of ill-doing, nor dreamed*
> *That any did. (I.ii.85-90)*

Polixenes says that had they not taken on the desires and responsibilities of adulthood, they would have remained guiltless before heaven of any inherited stain. What we have here is a doctrine of original innocence rather than original sin.

Perdita, the daughter of Hermione and Leontes, could be the personification of original innocence. Abandoned to the elements but rescued by a kind shepherd, she grows up in idyllic pastoral simplicity in Bohemia. At the age of sixteen, she falls in love with Florizel, who happens to be the son of King Polixenes. To escape Polixenes' wrath at his son's betrothal to a mere shepherd's daughter, they flee to Sicilia.

Back in Sicilia, Leontes has suffered terrible remorse for sixteen years, weeping and making regular visits to the tombs of Hermione and his son. Perdita and Florizel arrive at Leontes' court, pursued by the angry Polixenes. But Perdita's identity is soon revealed, and Perdita, Leontes, and Polixenes happily reconcile. At last, Paulina leads them to a gallery containing what appears to be a statue of Hermione. On seeing it, Leontes' says:

> *I am ashamed. Does not the stone rebuke me*
> *For being more stone than it? (V.iii.37-38)*

Perdita kneels for blessing before her mother's statue, which comes to life, warmly embraces Leontes, and blesses Perdita, saying:

> *You gods, look down,*
> *And from your sacred vials pour your graces*
> *Upon my daughter's head! (V.iii.153-155)*

A jealous rage turned Leontes' heart to stone, and his monstrous behavior left his wife and children as lifeless as his heart, or so he thought. After sixteen years of remorse, what was thought to be stone comes to life. Although his son is lost, Leontes finds grace in the restoration of a living wife and daughter.

Remorse is the part of one who has done wrong. Forgiveness is the part of one who has suffered wrong. Forgiveness is the subject of our next chapter.

18

Forgiveness

WHEN WE WON'T FORGIVE, we are trapped in thoughts of the past and suffer from negative emotions of resentment and anger. We break free of this trap when we let go of such thoughts and dwell mindfully in the present. In the words of the Buddha:

"Look how he abused me and beat me,
How he threw me down and robbed me."
Live with such thoughts and you live in hate.
"Look how he abused me and beat me,
How he threw me down and robbed me."
Abandon such thoughts and live in love.[71]

A wise person once said that "Forgiveness means giving up all hope of a better past." And giving up all hope of a better past frees the mind from negative emotions.

Measure for Measure presents a stark contrast between harsh judgment and forgiveness. As the play opens, the Duke of Vienna deputizes Angelo to rule in his absence and then disguises himself as a friar to observe what follows. Once in power, Angelo enforces a neglected law against fornication, condemning to death one Claudio, who has gotten his contracted but not yet married spouse with child. Claudio turns to his sister, Isabella, a novice nun, to plead for his life. In response to her plea, Angelo offers to spare Claudio, but only if Isabella agrees to sleep with him. *Measure for Measure* is as contemporary as the latest revelations of sexual harassment in high places.

The disguised Duke visits Isabella and has her pretend to agree to Angelo's indecent proposal. He then sends Angelo's neglected fiancée, Mariana, to keep the assignation in Isabella's place. Thinking he has slept with Isabella, Angelo reneges on his promise and orders Claudio's execution. The Duke of Vienna secretly intervenes to save Claudio but lets the other characters think Claudio has been executed.

When the Duke throws off his disguise and returns to the court. Isabella seeks justice for her

executed brother, and the Duke hands down
Angelo's sentence:

> *An Angelo for Claudio, death for death!'*
> *Haste still pays haste, and leisure answers leisure;*
> *Like doth quit like, and measure still for meas-*
> *ure. (V.i.465-467)*

Mariana, now Angelo's wife, pleads for his life
and asks Isabella to join her. Isabella kneels be-
side Mariana, saying:

> *Look, if it please you, on this man condemn'd,*
> *As if my brother lived: I partly think*
> *A due sincerity govern'd his deeds,*
> *Till he did look on me: since it is so,*
> *Let him not die. (V.i.509-513)*

Isabella pleads for the life of a man she has
every reason to hate, just as she pleaded for the
life of the brother she loves. When the living
Claudio appears, Angelo is pardoned.

Isabella's act of forgiveness in pleading for the
life of Angelo is extraordinary. She forgives the
man who sought to violate her innocence and,
thinking he had done so, tries to kill the brother
he had promised to spare. It would be hard to

imagine a greater triumph of forgiveness over the natural desire for judgement. The title of the play is from a verse in the *Sermon on the Mount:*

> *For with what judgment ye judge, ye shall be judged, and with what measure ye mete, it shall be measured unto you again. (Matthew 7:2)*

The Buddha gives similar advice:

> *Do not be the judge of people; do not make assumptions about others. A person is destroyed by holding judgments about others.*[72]

While judgment will come, it belongs to the Lord for Christians and Jews and to karma for Buddhists. It belongs to us to take care of our minds and forgive.

. . .

In *The Tempest*, probably the last play he wrote without a co-author, Shakespeare leaves us with another demonstration of forgiveness. Prospero, Duke of Milan, has much to forgive. Deposed by his brother, Antonio, with the help of Alonso, Duke of Naples, he is cast away in a leaky boat with his infant daughter, Miranda. They wash up on an enchanted island inhabited by Caliban, the half-human son of a witch. Using magic powers attained through long study, Prospero subdues Caliban and rules the island.

During the play, Prospero – assisted by his attendant spirit, Ariel, uses his magic to:

- Raise a tempest that appears to destroy a ship containing his enemies and their entourage,
- Miraculously bring the ship's passengers, including Antonio, Alonso, and Alonso's innocent son, Ferdinand, to the island unharmed,
- Foil murderous plots hatched by Antonio, Caliban, and others,
- Arrange for Miranda and Ferdinand to fall in love, and
- Summon a masque of spirits to celebrate their marriage.

Having worked his spells and with his enemies in his power, Prospero's thoughts turn from revenge to reconciliation:

> *Though with their high wrongs I am struck to th'*
> *quick,*
> *Yet with my nobler reason 'gainst my fury*

Do I take part. The rarer action is
In virtue than in vengeance. They being penitent,
The sole drift of my purpose doth extend
Not a frown further. (V.i.34-39)

He embraces his former enemies in a general welcome. There is a joyful reunion of Alonso and Ferdinand, who have thought one another drowned. And Prospero and Alonso join in mutual happiness at the forthcoming marriage of their children. When Alonso asks forgiveness, Prospero responds:

There, sir, stop.
Let us not burden our remembrances with
A heaviness that's gone. (V.i.236-238)

Prospero renounces the practice of magic, frees Ariel, forgives the plotters, and pardons Caliban as he prepares to return as Duke to Milan. While Prospero has been generous in forgiving his former enemies, he may also need forgiveness, having used occult powers to control the other characters. In the epilogue, he invites members of the audience to remember their culpability and extend the forgiveness that he needs:

And my ending is despair,
Unless I be relieved by prayer,
Which pierces so that it assaults
Mercy itself and frees all faults.
As you from crimes would pardoned be,
Let your indulgence set me free. (Epi.15-20)

Not all of Shakespeare's malefactors seek or receive forgiveness. No one forgives the unrepentant Richard III, Macbeth, Iago, Claudius, or Edmund. But in *The Tempest*, Shakespeare leaves us with a reminder that if we want forgiveness, we must be ready to forgive.

When wronged, we often let ego chime in and make it about us. But listening to ego will do nothing to undo the wrong and will only "burden our remembrance with a heaviness that's gone." If instead we realize that it's not about us, we can regard the other person with an equal mind, recognizing that, whatever their delusions, they want to be happy just as we do. Then we can forgive and free our minds of anger and resentment. Although they suffered terrible wrongs, Isabella and Prospero overruled their egos, let go of the past, and unburdened their minds. Egolessness is the subject of our next chapter.

19

Egolessness

E GOLESSNESS OR NOT-SELF (anatta) signifies the lack of intrinsic existence in self and phenomena. It is the third characteristic of existence taught by the Buddha.[73] As he told his followers:

> *The thought of self is an error, and all existences are as hollow as the plantain tree and as empty as twirling water bubbles.*[74]

If we want to appreciate egolessness as it applies to our selves, we can start by asking who we would be without our bodily form, thoughts, emotions, relationships, possessions, skills, reputation, strength, opinions, beliefs, position in society, etc. These aspects of our ego identity, and any others that we can imagine, are impermanent and without intrinsic existence. The self to which we cling is a set of concepts based on transient phenomena.

If we could stop clinging to the false notion of a solid self, we would realize that we have spent our lives constructing an ephemeral *"me"* while overlooking our true nature, our buddha-nature or luminous mind, which we share with all beings. Out of such a realization would come a healthy sense of self-worth. We would act with care and compassion for others still struggling with false notions of ego identity. And we would be free of the burden of protecting aspects of an identity that is without intrinsic existence. With such freedom, we might find openness and clarity. But, sadly, this is not where most of us are. For most of us, losing one or two cherished aspects of our ego-identity would be a shattering experience. Some of Shakespeare's characters find themselves in this very position.

Consider Richard II. Indulgent with his friends and profligate with money, Richard goes too far when he exiles his cousin, Henry Bolingbroke, and seizes his assets to pay for wars in Ireland. Henry returns from exile at the head of an invading army, and Richard returns from Ireland to find that his friends have fled, been killed, or gone over to Bolingbroke. Before realizing that all is lost, he clings to his identity as a divinely elected monarch:

> *Not all the water in the rough rude sea*
> *Can wash the balm off from an anointed king;*
> *(III.ii.55-56)*

When it becomes clear that he must submit to his cousin, he imagines himself exchanging the trappings of kingship for the identity of a humble monk:

> *I'll give my jewels for a set of beads,*
> *My gorgeous palace for a hermitage,*
> *My gay apparel for an almsman's gown,*
> *My figured goblets for a dish of wood,*
> *My scepter for a palmer's walking-staff,*
> *My subjects for a pair of carvèd saints,*
> *And my large kingdom for a little grave,*
> *(III.iii.152-158)*

He finds that the descent from power is not going to be that easy. Asked if he is ready to surrender the crown, he responds in distress:

> *Ay, no; no, ay; for I must nothing be. (IV.i.210)*

He cannot yet conceive of an existence as anything other than a king and sees no alternative but to be nothing. Once he has given up the crown, he no longer knows who he is and wishes that he could dissolve into oblivion:

> *I have no name, no title,*
> *No, not that name was given me at the font,*
> *But 'tis usurped. Alack the heavy day,*
> *That I have worn so many winters out*
> *And know not now what name to call myself.*
> *O, that I were a mockery king of snow*
> *Standing before the sun of Bolingbroke,*
> *To melt myself away in water drops. (IV.i.266-273)*

Sent to prison, Richard has these last thoughts before he dies at the hands of his enemies:

> *Sometimes am I king.*
> *Then treasons make me wish myself a beggar,*
> *And so I am; then crushing penury*
> *Persuades me I was better when a king.*
> *Then am I kinged again, and by and by*
> *Think that I am unkinged by Bolingbroke,*
> *And straight am nothing. But whate'er I be,*
> *Nor I nor any man that but man is*
> *With nothing shall be pleased till he be eased*
> *With being nothing. (V.v.32-41)*

134

Earlier, the thought that "I must nothing be" brought a cry of anguish from Richard. But in his last moments, he sees that only "with being nothing," only by letting go of attachment to identity, will he "be eased."

Shakespeare returns to the subject of royal identity in *King Lear*. Lear voluntarily gives up power to his daughters with the expectation that he will retain "the name and all addition to a king." He foolishly thinks he can give up power and keep the identity that goes with it but finds out otherwise when he goes to live with his daughter, Goneril. Instead of treating him like a king and beloved father, she bitterly scolds him for the behavior of his followers. His sense of identity shaken; Lear asks:

> *Does any here know me? This is not Lear.*
> *Does Lear walk thus, speak thus? Where are his eyes?*
> *Either his notion weakens, his discernings*
> *Are lethargied — Ha! Waking? 'Tis not so.*
> *Who is it that can tell me who I am? (I.iv.231-235)*

The Fool replies, "Lear's shadow." He knows that the identity for which Lear is searching is like a shadow. It appears but has no existence of its own. But Lear is not yet ready to "be eased with being nothing." The descent continues as his retinue is reduced by half and then taken away altogether. Left out in a storm with his sanity slipping away, he faces the loss of all that has defined his existence. Adrift and desperate to know who he is, he sees a naked beggar in the storm and exclaims:

Thou art the thing itself; unaccommodated man is no more but such a poor, bare, forked animal as thou art. (III.iv.114-115)

Then, with the storm raging around him, Lear begins tearing off his clothes, crying, "off, off you lendings!" It is as if he is trying to tear away aspects of his old identity that are causing him pain. Lear declines further into madness, obsessing about kingship, authority, and the ingratitude of children.

Cordelia returns from France to take him into her care, and she tries to reclaim the kingdom for him. But her forces are defeated in battle, and Lear and Cordelia are led away to prison. Only then does he finally appear to let go of attachment to power and position. As he consoles Cordelia, Lear sounds like a man who has emerged from darkness into light:

Come, let's away to prison:
We two alone will sing like birds i' the cage:
When thou dost ask me blessing, I'll kneel down,
And ask of thee forgiveness: so we'll live,
And pray, and sing, and tell old tales, and laugh
At gilded butterflies, and hear poor rogues
Talk of court news; and we'll talk with them too,
Who loses and who wins; who's in, who's out;
And take upon's the mystery of things,
As if we were God's spies: and we'll wear out,
In a wall'd prison, packs and sects of great ones,
That ebb and flow by the moon. (V.iii.9-20)

Having let go of attachments that have defined his identity, Lear gains a new understanding. He now knows that his lost power and position were ephemeral, like the "packs and sects of great ones that ebb and flow by the moon." Unencumbered by old burdens, he is ready for a carefree existence as one of "God's spies." Unhappily, Cordelia is murdered in prison, and with her death, Lear again falls into anguish. But at the very end, he dies under the apparent impression that Cordelia lives.

After much suffering, Richard II and King Lear glimpse the truth. Richard knows at the end that our suffering is relieved only when we are "eased with being nothing," with letting go of attachment to identity. And Lear envisions, if only for a moment, the contentment to be found in freedom from self, living as a hermit, and considering "the mystery of things."

As we have seen, the ego can be like a house of cards. When a cherished aspect of ego identity is removed, the whole thing collapses. This leaves a character like Richard II or King Lear struggling to know who they are. Such a character can go into denial, like Richard II, or go mad, like Lear. But in both cases, the loss of identity clears the way for the emergence of a healthier sense of self. Unfortunately, this breakthrough is soon followed by the character's death.

Shakespeare shows what can happen when we cling to an ego that is balanced precariously on a set of false assumptions about our identity. But was Shakespeare himself without ego-clinging? That is the subject of our final chapter.

20

Was Shakespeare Egoless?

I F SHAKESPEARE HAD egoistic attachments, they left few traces in his plays. We cannot draw from them any firm conclusions about his personal preferences, opinions, or beliefs. While John Milton used poetry to "justify the ways of God to men," Shakespeare had no such agendas. The opinions and beliefs we find in his plays are those of the characters, not the playwright. Shakespeare is like the artist described by James Joyce in *A Portrait of the Artist as a Young Man*, who:

> *remains within or behind or beyond or above his handiwork, invisible, refined out of existence.*[75]

He is like the presence Virginia Woolf sensed when she visited Shakespeare's grave in Stratford and wrote in her diary:

> *He is serenely absent-present; both at once; radiating around one; . . . but never to be pinned down.*[76]

William Hazlitt, Ralph Waldo Emerson, and John Keats all remarked on Shakespeare's lack of ego. Hazlitt wrote:

> *He (Shakespeare) was the least of an egoist that it was possible to be; he was nothing in himself, but he was all that others were or could become.*[77]

Emerson, who had read Hazlitt's essays, expressed a similar view:

> *Shakespeare has no peculiarity, no importunate topic, but all is duly given. He has no discoverable egotism.*[78]

John Keats was also familiar with Hazlitt's opinion and shared it. He even coined the term *negative capability* to describe the remarkable quality that he found in Shakespeare. He explains in a letter to his brothers:

> *At once it struck me, what quality went to form a man of achievement especially in literature & which Shakespeare possessed so enormously – I mean Negative Capability, that is when man is capable of being in uncertainties, mysteries, doubts, without any irritable reaching after fact & reason.*[79]

140

Negative capability is openness to experience without needing to question, understand, or control. It is a quality that a person with "no discoverable egotism" would possess.

The Buddhist teacher and author, Stephen Batchelor, compares negative capability to "the practice of Zen Buddhism."[80] Considering the statement that Shakespeare "was nothing in himself, but he was all that others were or could become," Batchelor suggests that it could describe the awakened Buddha sitting under the bodhi tree.[81]

The ability to be present with life in all its mystery, unburdened by attachments, is an ability that the Buddha exemplifies. If Keats, Hazlitt, Emerson, and Batchelor are right and Shakespeare possessed it, then he resembled the Buddha in this respect.

Not that we have to think of Shakespeare as a holy man to appreciate his genius. Perhaps he had attachments like most of us. His sonnets and what we know of his life suggest that this was the case. But when he sat down to write his plays, he set attachments aside and entered a creative space of openness and clarity. Thus unencumbered, his mind became a polished mirror, reflecting human nature in all its variety. We find the mirror metaphor in Hamlet's speech to the players:

> *the purpose of playing . . . is, to hold as t'were the mirror up to nature, to show virtue her own feature, scorn her own image, and the very age and body of the time his form and pressure. (III.ii.23-26)*

From Shakespeare's mirror-like mind came poetry and dramatic situations that illustrate truths taught by the Buddha. In some passages, we may even glimpse the openness and clarity that lie beyond the false sense of a separate self. When we experience Shakespeare's plays and poems, we are often in the presence of universal wisdom, reflected in a polished mirror and resonating with the teachings of the Buddha.

Appendix: Meditate with Shakespeare

As we saw in our chapter on mindfulness, Shakespeare's works are grounded in mindful attention to outer and inner phenomena. Such observation is itself a form of meditation. To the extent that we can quiet distracting thoughts and emotions and observe what goes on around and within us, we are following the example of Shakespeare, the mindfulness meditator.

In addition to following Shakespeare's example, we can join with him in a simple, introductory practice of meditation. We do this by choosing as the object of our meditation a passage or a part of a passage that resonates with us and with the Dharma. We might take the first two lines of *Sonnet 60* as a meditation on impermanence.

> Like as the waves make towards the pebbled shore,
> So do our minutes hasten to their end.

- To begin, sit comfortably with back straight and eyes open or half open, looking down or straight ahead. Arouse gratitude for all sources of wisdom and inspiration and wish that all beings might benefit.
- Be aware of the breath as you breathe in and out.
- When you feel settled, read the words of the passage, reflecting on their meaning.
- Then, for the main part of the practice, say the lines silently to yourself. Synchronize the words and the breath in a way that captures the rhythm of the poetry for you. You might, for instance, say "Like as the waves" on the in-breath, "make toward the pebbled shore" on the outbreath, and "so do our minutes" on the inbreath, "hasten to their end," on the outbreath.
- While repeating the words to yourself, let them wash over and through you like waves advancing toward the shore. Focus on the rhythm and sound of the words.
- If you are distracted, just return your attention to the breath and the words of the passage. If you feel drowsy, you might try saying the words aloud for a while.

146

- When it is time to conclude your practice, re-member again to be grateful for all true sources of wisdom and inspiration and wish that all beings might benefit from them..

Meditating on a few words or lines from Shake-speare can be a variation on *mantra* meditation. In Sanskrit, *mantra* means a sacred message or syllables that protect the mind. For some of us, mantras can even be found in the works of Shakespeare and other poets. But meditation on Shakespeare's words is not a substitute for more traditional mantras, which are said to have spe-cial transformative powers. Shakespeare's works are just one of countless sources of inspiration.

Below are a few brief passages that could serve as objects of meditation. They illustrate themes common to both Shakespeare and Buddhism.

Non-attachment

Let be. (Hamlet)

Our content is our best having. (Henry VIII)

Egolessness, Not-Self

Who is it that can tell me who I am? (King Lear)

Mind

There is nothing either good or bad but thinking makes it so. (Hamlet)

Impermanence & death

Man's life's no more than to say 'one.' (Hamlet)

The rest is silence. (Hamlet)

Illusion

We are such stuff
As dreams are made on, and our little life
Is rounded with a sleep. (The Tempest)

All the world's a stage,
And all the men and women merely players.
(As You Like It)

Compassion

O, I have suffered
With those that I saw suffer! (The Tempest)

Poor naked wretches, wheresoe'er you are,
That bide the pelting of this pitiless storm.

(King Lear)

Reading Suggestions

Pema Chodron, *When Things Fall Apart*

Ani Tenzin Palmo, *Reflections on a Mountain Lake*

Jack Kornfield, *A Path With Heart: A Guide Through the Perils and Promises of Spiritual Life*

Mingyur Rinpoche, *The Joy of Living: Unlocking the Secret and Science of Happiness*

Chogyam Trungpa, *Cutting Through Spiritual Materialism*

Joseph Goldstein, *One Dharma*

Matthieu Ricard, Why Meditate

Dzogchen Ponlop, *Rebel Buddha: On the Road to Freedom*

Achaan Chah, A Still Forest Pool

Sharon Salzberg, *Lovingkindness: The Revolutionary Art of Happiness*

Sogyal Rinpoche, *The Tibetan Book of Living and Dying*

Toknyi Rinpoche, Open Hears, Open Mind

Shunryu Suzuki, Zen Mind Beginners Mind

Thich Nhat Hanh, The Miracle of Mindfulness

Acknowledgements

OVER THE PAST QUARTER CENTURY, I have heard and read many Buddhist teachings. For most of these years my main teacher was Sogyal Rinpoche, who may have been the first Buddhist teacher to use examples from Shakespeare. Many of the insights and examples in this book were first encountered in his teachings. I am deeply grateful to him and to all who have devoted their lives to generously sharing the Buddhist Dharma.

For many of the Buddha's sayings, I have drawn on *The Dhammapada* as translated by Thomas Byrom. For translations of the word of the Buddha from other sources, I am indebted to Access to Insight, The Buddhist Publication Society, and The Oxford Pali Text Society. For translations of passages from teachers in the lineages of Tibetan Buddhism, I am indebted to the Rigpa Shedra. My sources for stories from the life of the Buddha have been *The Awakened One: A Life of the Buddha* by Sherab Chodzin Kohn and *The Teachings of the Buddha*, edited by Jack Kornfield and Gil Fronsdal.

My source for passages from Shakespeare's works is Folger Digital Texts, available at: https://shakespeare.folger.edu/shakespeares-works. In a few cases, next to the words most likely to be unfamiliar, I have placed a modern equivalent in brackets.

All sources are cited in the endnotes. *Shakespeare Meets the Buddha* is a scholarly project published under the category of Shakespearean Literary Criticism. It is intended to highlight affinities between the Buddhist Dharma and the works of Shakespeare.The project is non-commercial. Any income from book sales, over and above printing, distribution, and promotion costs, will be donated to not-for-profit organizations engaged in sharing Buddhist teachings or in performing Shakespeare's plays.

Author

Edward Dickey is retired from a thirty-year career at the National Endowment for the Arts, where he was Director of the State & Regional Program. While earning an M.A. in Lit-  erature from American University, he was a junior fellow with the Folger Institute at the Folger Shakespeare Library. He has spent a lifetime studying and enjoying Shakespeare's plays and has been active with a local Dharma group for 24 years. He lives in Washington, D.C.

Notes

---

[1] Om Mani Padme Hung is the mantra of the Buddha of Compassion. It translates into English as "the jewel is in the lotus."

[2] The description of my meditation retreat in the first chapter is a composite of retreat experiences in France and the United States.

[3] The Deer Park at Sarnath, near the Ganges in India, is the location where the Buddha taught the Four Noble Truths. It was his first teaching.

[4] Nirvana is a state beyond concept that transcends suffering.

[5] Jonson, Ben. *To the Memory of My Beloved, The Author, Mr. William Shakespeare*, Poetry Foundation, 2016 (07/19/2016) http://www.poetryfoundation.org/poems-and- poets/poems/detail/44466

[6] Foakes, R.A., Coleridge on Shakespeare: *The Text of the Lectures of 1811-12.* (London & New York: Routledge, 2013) p. 166.

[7] Coleridge, Samuel Taylor, *The Table Talk and Omniana of Samuel Taylor Coleridge* (London: George Bell and Sons, 1884) p. 278.

[8] "Myriad-minded." *Merriam-Webster.com Dictionary*, Merriam-Webster, https://www.merriam-webster.com/dictionary/myriad-minded. Accessed 22 Apr. 2024.

[9] My source for passages from Shakespeare's works is Folger Digital Texts. https://www.folger.edu/explore/shakespeares-works/

[10] Jon Kabat-Zinn, *Defining Mindfulness, Mindful: Healthy Living Healthy Life*, 11 Jan. 2017 (01 Mar 2019) https://www.mindful.org/jon-kabat-zinn-defining-mindfulness/

[11] Thomas Byrom, *The Dhammapada: The Sayings of the Buddha* (Boston: Shambhala Publications, 1993) p. 9.

[12] Hazlitt, *William, Shakespeare and Milton* (New York: W.W. Norton & Company, 1923) p. 2.

[13] https://www.rspb.org.uk/birds-and-wildlife/wildlife-guides/bird-a-z/lapwing/

[14] Laura Forbes. Elephant Journal. December 1 2015. *People Watching is the New Meditation*. https://www.elephantjournal.com/2015/12/people-watching-is-the-new-meditation/

[15] Open Source Shakespeare, Shakespeare Text Statistics https://www.opensourceshakespeare.org/statistics/

[16] Thomas Byrom, *The Dhammapada: The Sayings of the Buddha* (Boston: Shambhala Publications, 1993) p. 1

[17] Ibid. p. 13

[18] Geshe Langri Tangpa, *Eight Verses of Training the Mind*, Rigpa Shedra, 27 Apr. 2016 (15Jun2016) http://www.rigpawiki.org/index.php?title=Eight_Verses_of_Training_the_Mind

[19] The Buddha, *Dhammacakkappavattana Sutta: Setting Rolling the Wheel of Truth from the Samyutta Nikaya*, Nanamoli Thera, trans. 13 June 2010 (03 Mar 2019) https://www.accesstoinsight.org/tipitaka/sn/sn56/sn56.011.nymo.html

[20] Ethan Anderson, *Lincoln: Shakespeare's Greatest Character*, 08 Dec. 2020 (27 Jan. 2021) https://www.neh.gov/blog/lincoln-shakespeares-greatest-character

[21] *Three Types of Suffering.* Rigpa Shedra 23 June 2019 (27 August 2023) https://www.rigpawiki.org/index.php?title=Three_types_of_suffering

[22] https://www.rigpawiki.org/index.php?title=Quotations:_Shantideva,_Bodhicharyavatara,_Though_longing_to_be_rid_of_suffering...

[23] *Three Types of Suffering.* Rigpa Shedra 23 June 2019 (27 August 2023) https://www.rigpawiki.org/index.php?title=Three_types_of_suffering

[24] Ibid.

[25] Alongside attachment and aversion, Buddhists sometimes include indifference, which is a dull state of not

caring. Such indifference or intentional lack of engagement also arises out of ignorance. It is a negative state and not to be confused with equanimity or non-attachment.

[26] *Samyutta Nikaya 36:21. Collected Discourses of the Buddha,* translated by Bhikkhu Bodhi (Somerville, MA: Wisdom Publications, 2000) p.1278

[27] Thich Nhat Hanh, *The Four Immeasurable Minds,* Winter 1997 (Feb 2022) https://www.mindfulnessbell.org/archive/2016/01/dharma-talk-the-four-immeasurable-minds-

[28] Santideva. The Bodhicaryavatara. Kate Crosby and Andrew Skelton trans. 1995 (Oxford University Press) p. 99

[29] Goddard, Harold C. *The Meaning of Shakespeare, Volume 2.* (Chicago; University of Chicago Press, 1951) p. 69.

[30] Sogyal Rinpoche. *The Tibetan Book of Living and Dying.* (Harper San Francisco, 2001) p. 202.

[31] Shakespeare can only give us soon-to-be nuptials because the law did not allow weddings or other sacred ceremonies to be depicted onstage. So, the comedies often end with music and dancing,

[32] Life's Highest Blessings: The Maha Mangala Sutra. Dr. R.L. Soni, trans. (Kandy Sri Lanka: Buddhist Publication Society, 1956), 86.

[33] Buddha Shakyamuni. *Metta Sutta: Loving-kindness*, Nanamoli Thera, trans. https://www.accesstoinsight.org/tipitaka/an/an04/an04.125.nymo.html (1998)

[34] Even Shakespeare's least sympathetic characters, including Richard III and Iago, are more than pasteboard villains. They are complex but severely deluded human beings.

[35] Pema Chodron. *Comfortable with Uncertainty* (Boston: Shambhala Publications, 2008) p. 77.

[36] Yogacara Bhumi Sutra from Edward Conze (ed.) *Buddhist Texts through the Ages* (Boston: Shambhala Publications, 1990), found in *The Teachings of the Buddha*, Jack Kornfield, ed., (Boston: Shambhala Publications, 1993) p. 16.

[37] Maha-parinibbana Sutta: Last Days of the Buddha. Sister Vajiri & Francis Story, trans. 1998. https://www.accesstoinsight.org/tipitaka/dn/dn.16.1-6.vaji.html

[38] Shunryu Suzuku. *Zen Mind, Beginner's Mind* (New York: Weatherhill,1970), 102-103. Note: Weatherhill is now an imprint of Shambhala Publications.

[39] Buddha Shakyamuni, *Dhammacakkappavattana Sutta: Setting Rolling the Wheel of Truth from the Samyutta Nikaya*, Nanamoli Thera, trans. 13 June 2010 (03 Mar 2019) https://www.accesstoinsight.org/tipitaka/sn/sn56/sn56.011.nymo.html

[40] Buddha Shakyamuni. *Lalitavistara Sutra*. Rigpa Shedra, 19 Nov. 2011 (22 Aug. 2016) http://www.rigpawiki.org

[41] Shakespeare's Writings Indicate He May Have Had Syphilis. Science Daily (January 11, 2005) https://www.sciencedaily.com/releases/2005/01/050111091800.htm

[42] Josh Jones, *74 Ways Characters Die in Shakespeare's Plays*. Open Culture 01 Jan 2016 (26 May 2016) http://www.openculture.com/2016/01/74-ways-characters-die-in-shakespeares-plays-shown-in-a-handy-infographic.html

[43] From the *Mahahaparinirvana Sutra*. Quoted in Sushila Blackman, *Graceful Exits: How Great Beings Die*.(Boston: Shambhala Publications,1993) p. 21.

[44] Milarepa, *In Horror of Death*. Rigpa Wiki. 27 December, 2015. (09 August, 2016) http://www.rigpawiki.org/index.php?title=Quotations:_Milarepa,_In_horror_of_death…

[25] Thich Nhat Hanh, Dharma Talk given by Thich Nhat Hanh on December 4, 1997 in Plum Village. (26 May 2016) http://www.buddhist-canon.com/PLAIN/TNHSUTTA/1997%20Dec%204%20%20Diamond%20Sutra%20(part%201).htm

[46] Heraclitus https://en.wikiquote.org/wiki/Heraclitus

[47] *The Diamond Sutra and the Sutra of Hui-neng*. A. F. Price and Wong Mou-lam trans., (Boston: Shambhala Publications, 1990) p. 146

[48] Buddha Shakyamuni. The King of Samadhhis Sutra. Peter Alan Roberts Trans. (84000: Translating the Words ob the Buddha, 2018) https://www.rigpawiki.org/index.php?title=King_of_Samadhi_Sutra

[49] Sherab Chodzin Kohn, *The Awakened One: A Life of the Buddha* (Boston: Shambhala Publications, 2000) p. 86.

[50] Quanta Magazine. *To Pay Attention, the Brain Uses Filters, Not a Spotlight.* (Aug 2023) https://www.quantamagazine.org/to-pay-attention-the-brain-uses-filters-not-a-spotlight-20190924/

[51] Dr. Robert Puff on The Enlightenment Podcast interprets the opening lines of the *Seven Ages of Man* soliloquy as a teaching on enlightenment. http://www.enlightenmentpodcast.com/what-shakespeare-can-teach-us-about-enlightenment-all-the-worlds-a-stage/

A Buddhist perspective on *Shakespeare's All the World's a Stage* was the subject of posts on the tiny buddha online forum: tiny buddha: simple wisdom for complex lives, (July 12, 2013) https://tinybuddha.com/topic/all-the-worlds-a-stage/

[52] Buddha Shakyamuni. *Pabhasarra Sutra: Luminous.* Thanissaro Bhikkhu trans. 1995. (05-02-2021) https://www.accesstoinsight.org/tipitaka/an/an01/an01.049.than.html

[53] I first encountered the analogy of the light bulb in a movie projector in teachings by Sogyal Rinpoche. The

analogy is also used by Venerable Tenzin Palmo in *Reflections on a Mountain Lake: Teachings on Practical Buddhism.* (Snow Lion Publications, 2002)

54 International Thomas Merton Society, The Merton Tapes, tape 8, side B, "Life & Solitude". A passage from an informal talk Merton gave in 1965. (https://www.facebook.com/groups/MERTON/posts/10158254496643311/ Jan. 2020)

55 Sigalovada Sutta. Narada Thera, trans.1996 (06-04-2024) https://www.accesstoinsight.org/tipitaka/dn/dn.31.0.nara.html335

56 Nick Bottom the Weaver garbles verses from Paul's Epistle to the Corinthians: "Eye hath not seen, nor ear heard, neither have entered into the heart of man, the things that God hath prepared for them that love him." (1 Corinthians 2:9-11)

57 Thomas Byrom, *The Dhammapada: The Sayings of the Buddha* (Boston: Shambhala Publications, 1993) p. 83.

58 Quoted in *David R. Loy, A Buddhist History of the West: Studies in Lack* (Albany: State University of New York Press, 2002) p. 209.

59 Sherab Chodzin Kohn, *The Awakened One: A Life of the Buddha* (Boston, Shambhala Publications, 2000) p. 78.

60 Thomas Byrom, *The Dhammapada: The Sayings of the Buddha* (Boston: Shambhala Publications, 1993) p. 36.

[61] Thomas Hardy, *The Dynasts*, (Part II, Scene V) 01 Sep 2013 (26 May 2016)

http://www.gutenberg.org/files/4043/4043-h/4043-h.html

[62] *Mahatanhasankhaya Sutta: The Greater Craving-Destruction Discourse*. Thanissaro Bikkhu trans., 2011. (May2019) https://www.accesstoinsight.org/tipitaka/mn/mn.038.than.html

[63] Thich Nhat Hanh. *The Heart of Understanding* (Berkeley California: Parallax Press, 1988) pp. 3-4.

[64] Descriptions of the twelve links of interdependent origination can be found online, including at the following address: https://www.rigpawiki.org/index.php?title=Twelve_links_of_dependent_origination

[65] Padmasambhava, *Quotations: Padsambhava*, Rigpa Shedra, Dec 26, 2015 2019) https://www.rigpawiki.org/index.php?title=Quotations:_Padmasambhava,_Although_my_view_is_higher_than_the_sky...

[66] Thomas Byrom, *The Dhammapada: The Sayings of the Buddha* (Boston: Shambhala Publications, 1993) p. 35.

[67] Shakespeare and his contemporaries would have encountered the concept of rebirth or reincarnation in Greek Philosophy. In *Twelfth Nigh,t* the Clown asks Malvolio, "What is the opinion of Pythagoras concerning wild fowl?" and Malvolio responds, "That the soul of our grandam might haply inhabit a bird." (IV.ii.53)

[68] Thomas Byrom, *The Dhammapada: The Sayings of the Buddha* (Boston: Shambhala Publications, 1993), p. 84.

[69] Buddha-nature is the unstained and timeless nature of mind shared by all sentient beings.

[70] Sherab Chodzin Kohn, *The Awakened One: A Life of the Buddha* (Boston: Shambhala Publications, 2000), p. 98.

[71] Thomas Byrom, *The Dhammapada: The Sayings of the Buddha* (Boston: Shambhala Publications, 1993) p. 9.

[72] Anguttara Nikaya: *The Book of Gradual Sayings, Volume V*, F.L. Woodward and E.M. Hare, trans. (Oxford: Pali Text Society, 1994) p. 140.

[73] "Ego" can refer to a mistaken sense of self. For Buddhists, such an ego is a delusion because it is based on the false notion of an intrinsically existing self. "Ego" can also refer to a healthy sense of self-worth. Here the term is used in the negative sense of ego as delusion and "egolessness" as the lack of attachment to a false self.

[74] Henry Clarke Warren, (trans). *The Gospel of Buddha* (Chicago: Open Court, 1915) p. 18.

[75] James Joyce, *A Portrait of the Artist as a Young Man* (New York: The Viking Press, Inc.1964) p. 215.

[76] Virginia Stephen Woolf, *The Diary of Virginia Woolf, Volume Four 1931-1935.* (New York: Harcourt Brace Jovanovich, 1982) p. 219.

[77] *William Hazlitt, Essayist and Critic: Selections from His Writings.* (London: Frederick Warne and Co,1889) p. 113.

[78] Ralph Waldo Emerson. *The Prose Works of Ralph Waldo Emerson, Volume 2.* (Boston: James R. Osgood and Co,1876) p. 115.

[79] John Keats, *Selections from Keats' Letters (1817),* The Poetry Foundation 2016 https://www.poetryfoundation.org/resources/learning/essays/detail

[80] Stephen Batchelor. *The Practice of Negative Capability: Buddhist Reflections on Creative Uncertainty.* Sea of Faith. 2002 (27 May 2016) https://sofia.org.nz/2002batchelorkey.html

[81] Ibid.

Made in the USA
Middletown, DE
26 December 2024